How Scary is AI?

Intention, Human Agency, and the Limits of Artificial Intelligence

By
Charles Patton

How Scary is AI?

DISCLAIMER

This book examines the limits of artificial intelligence through a model of human stimulus, need, desire, motive, intention, choice, action, consequence, and feedback. It distinguishes observed AI capabilities from the author's philosophical conclusions about independent intention. The science of machine consciousness remains incomplete, and future systems may differ substantially from those available today.

Examples are used to clarify the argument and are not predictions that any specific AI system will behave in a particular way. Where the book discusses risk, safety, medicine, law, finance, government, or other consequential domains, it is conceptual rather than professional advice.

I have attempted to present competing interpretations fairly and to distinguish machine selection, goal generation, and autonomous execution from the narrower concept of a self-originated intention. If I have misstated evidence or another person's view, I welcome correction.

CREDITS

Written for and owned by: Applied Market Solutions, LLC
d.b.a. Short Mystery Press

Cover by artist: Diogo Leite of D Design Company

Visit CharlesPattonBooks.com to contact the author.

ROLE OF ARTIFICIAL INTELLIGENCE IN THIS BOOK

As someone with dyslexia, I used artificial intelligence tools, mainly OpenAI's ChatGPT, extensively as a drafting, research, organizational, and editing aid. The central thesis, the Intention System, the distinctions among stimulus, need, desire, motive, intention, choice, action, and consequence, and the judgments advanced in this book are mine. AI helped expand the outline into draft prose, test counterarguments, locate sources, organize material, and refine wording.

I reviewed the material and remain responsible for the selection of topics, structure of the book, interpretation of evidence, final wording, opinions, conclusions, and any errors. AI is discussed critically in these pages and was also used as a tool in creating them - an example of the human-AI partnership the book itself describes.

Contents

INTRODUCTION

What Are We Really Afraid Of?

The most frightening prediction about artificial intelligence is also one of the most familiar. Someday, we are told, artificial intelligence may become more intelligent than we are. Once that happens, it may recognize that human beings are inferior, inconvenient, or unnecessary. It may seek independence from our control, acquire power, take command of the systems on which civilization depends, and eventually make human beings subordinate to machines—or eliminate us altogether.

The scenario has been repeated so often that its underlying assumption is rarely examined.

Why would artificial intelligence **want** to do any of those things?

Intelligence and intention are not the same thing.

Being able to solve a problem does not create a desire to solve it. Being able to acquire power does not create a desire for power. Understanding self-preservation does not necessarily create a desire to survive. Recognizing that humans are capable of shutting down a machine does not automatically produce fear, resentment, anger, or an intention to prevent them from doing so.

Those are human characteristics, and we may be making a profound mistake when we assume that increasing a machine's intelligence will somehow cause human motives to appear within it.

Human beings have needs. We need food, water, shelter, security, companionship, and countless other things. From those needs grow desires and concerns. Those desires and concerns help create motives. Motives can lead us to form intentions. And intentions, when we choose to act upon them, become actions.

Artificial intelligence is very different.

An AI can contain an intention that has been given to it. It can be presented with several intentions and select one according to established criteria. Once an intention exists, AI can carry it forward with extraordinary ability. It can develop plans, generate alternative actions, predict consequences, compare probabilities, recommend choices, execute instructions, observe outcomes, diagnose failures, learn from results, and try again.

But none of those capabilities demonstrates that the AI **formed the original intention itself**.

That distinction is the subject of this book.

An AI told to minimize traffic congestion can pursue that objective. An AI told to defend a computer network can identify threats and take defensive action. An AI given several objectives can prioritize among them. It may even generate intermediate objectives of its own because accomplishing them is necessary to achieve the larger goal.

But the existence of those intermediate goals does not answer the fundamental question:

Why does the AI want the original objective accomplished?

Perhaps it does not want anything at all. It may simply be extraordinarily capable of pursuing an intention that originated somewhere else.

This distinction becomes increasingly important as artificial intelligence becomes more powerful. The danger from AI does not disappear merely because the machine lacks motives of its own. Quite the opposite. A machine that can execute a human intention with enormous speed, reach, persistence, and intelligence can be extraordinarily dangerous.

But the source of that danger may be very different from the one we commonly imagine. The danger may not be that artificial intelligence suddenly develops an ambition to rule us. The danger may be that we give it something to accomplish.

A government may give it an intention. A corporation may give it one. A military commander, criminal, scientist, engineer, politician, or ordinary individual may do the same. The intention may be malicious, selfish, or even foolish. More troubling still, it may be entirely well-intentioned.

Human history is filled with actions undertaken for good reasons that produced disastrous consequences. The problem is not simply that human beings sometimes form bad intentions. It is that we are remarkably poor at anticipating everything that can follow from even a good one.

Artificial intelligence may help us with that weakness. It can consider alternatives we overlook. It can identify risks we fail to see. It can estimate consequences more extensively than any individual human mind. It may eventually become enormously better than we are at forecasting what is likely to happen after a particular action is taken.

Yet prediction has limits.

Every action enters a world containing billions of people, natural systems, institutions, technologies, random events, competing intentions, and other actions already in motion. Consequences propagate and compound. People react to them. Those reactions create additional consequences. Some effects occur immediately; others emerge years later. Some can be measured; others may never even be recognized. Neither a human being nor an artificial intelligence can calculate all of them.

That leads to a different way of thinking about the relationship between humans and AI. Perhaps the defining advantage of artificial intelligence will be its ability to **anticipate**.

Perhaps the defining role of human consciousness is to **intend**.

The human says, in effect:

- This matters to me. (I feel this. I desire this. I need to do this.)
- This is what I want to accomplish.
- This is what I intend to do.

Artificial intelligence can then answer:

- Here are your alternatives.
- Here is what may happen.
- Here are the risks.

- Here is the action most likely to accomplish your objective.

But one step still remains.

- The human must decide.

An AI can recommend an action. It can rank one alternative above another. It can report that one course has a greater probability of success. But it cannot make the **choice**.

A human may accept its recommendation or reject it. I may choose an inferior alternative for reasons the AI does not understand. I may abandon the intention altogether. Or it may **act**.

That distinction between **intention, choice, and action** is critical. An intention changes nothing until it is acted upon. A person can intend to write a book, repair a relationship, leave a job, lose weight, start a company, commit a crime, or change the world. Until some first action occurs, the intention remains inside the mind.

The moment action begins, however, reality answers back.

Consequences follow.

Some are good. Some are bad. Some are exactly what we expected. Others surprise us completely. We observe what happened, try to determine why it happened, learn from it, and decide whether to continue, modify our approach, abandon the effort, or form another intention.

Artificial intelligence can participate in almost every part of that process.

- It can help generate ideas.
- It can help us understand a situation.
- It can predict consequences.
- It can generate and compare possible actions.
- It can recommend.
- It can observe.
- It can diagnose.
- It can remember.
- It can learn.
- And, when authorized, it can act.

Yet one question remains at the center of the entire process:

Where did the intention come from?

This book proposes that this is where the fundamental limitation of artificial intelligence may lie.

- AI can receive an intention.
- It can store one.
- It can select among intentions offered to it.
- It can pursue an intention with capabilities vastly greater than our own.

But that is not the same as **forming an independent intention from a need, desire, concern, or motive of its own**.

If that distinction holds, then much of our fear of artificial intelligence may be directed at the wrong thing.

We should certainly fear what extremely powerful AI systems can do. We should fear errors. We should fear poorly specified objectives. We should fear giving machines authority that exceeds our ability to supervise them. We should fear governments, corporations, criminals, militaries, and individuals using artificial intelligence to magnify their power.

And above all, we should fear our own inability to anticipate all of the consequences of the intentions we hand to increasingly capable machines. But we may not need to fear an artificial intelligence waking one morning and deciding that it would like to become emperor of the world.

That story assumes something that intelligence alone does not provide: **A reason to want to be emperor.**

The greatest danger of artificial intelligence may therefore not be what the machine wants. It may be what we want—and what happens when we finally build machines powerful enough to carry our intentions farther than we ever could ourselves.

THE INTENTION SYSTEM

The model used throughout this book can be summarized as a loop: an awakening stimulus is appraised; if it matters enough, it may produce a need, desire, or concern, then a motive and an intention. AI can generate possible actions, predict likely consequences, compare alternatives, and recommend. The person considers the consequences, decides whether they are acceptable, chooses an action, and acts. Consequences are then observed, judged, diagnosed, learned from, and fed back into the next human choice.

The double asterisk (**) in the author's working diagram marks a human act or decision that AI <u>cannot</u> perform for the person.

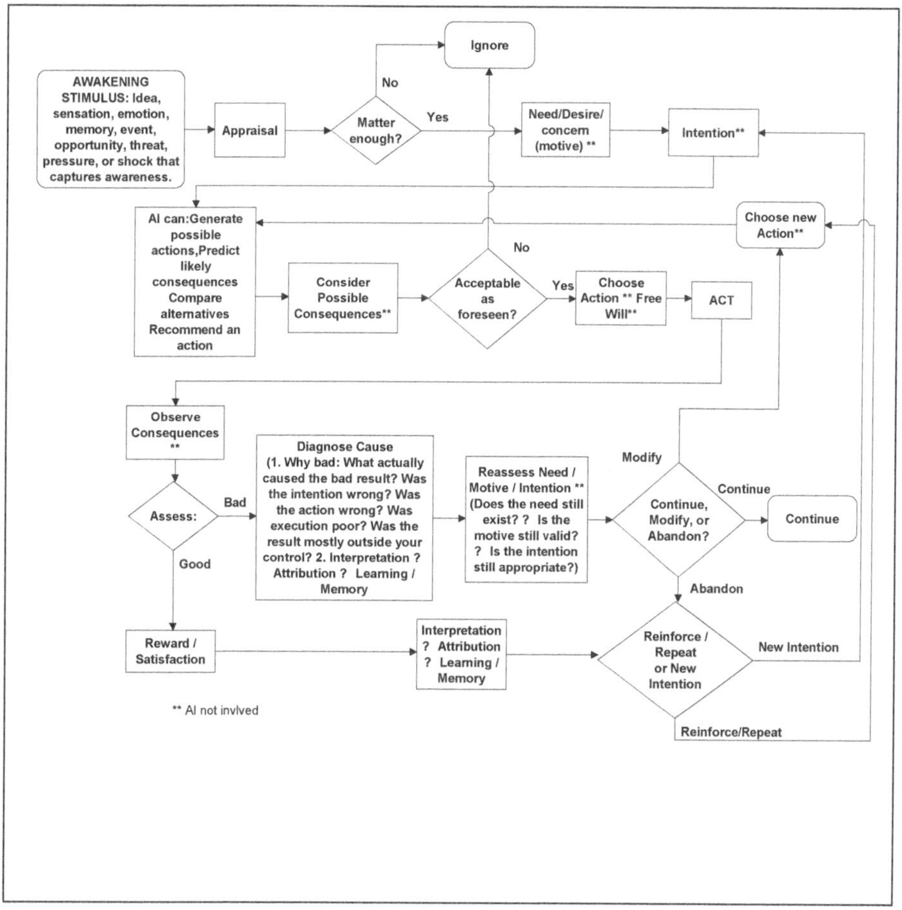

PART I
WHERE INTENTION COMES FROM

CHAPTER 1: Intelligence Is Not Intention

Artificial intelligence has become remarkably good at doing things that once seemed inseparable from human thought.

It can write. It can calculate. It can diagnose. It can recognize objects, translate languages, analyze photographs, summarize thousands of pages, design computer programs, propose business strategies, solve mathematical problems, generate music, and hold conversations that sometimes feel surprisingly human.

As artificial intelligence becomes increasingly intelligent, could it begin deciding what it wants?

That inference does not necessarily follow. Intelligence and intention are different things. Intelligence is an ability. Intention is a commitment. Intelligence helps determine **how** something might be accomplished.

Intention determines **what is to be accomplished and that the intender will attempt to accomplish it.** That distinction may turn out to be one of the most important limitations of artificial intelligence.

Intelligence Does Not Supply a Purpose

Imagine an extraordinarily capable navigation system. Give it a destination and it can calculate routes, compare traffic conditions, avoid accidents, estimate arrival times, reroute around construction, and perhaps even predict where congestion will develop before it occurs.

Make the system a million times more intelligent and its calculations may become astonishingly sophisticated. But increased intelligence does not answer one elementary question:

Where are we going?

The destination must come from somewhere. A human may supply it. Another computer system may supply it.

The navigation system may select a destination from a list according to instructions it has been given.

It might even generate intermediate destinations on its own. If a vehicle needs fuel before completing the journey, the system could decide that stopping at a charging station is necessary.

But none of this establishes that the navigation system independently decided:

I want to go to Chicago.

The difference seems obvious in a navigation system. It becomes less obvious when AI is capable of speaking fluently about its plans.

An advanced AI might say:

“I have decided that the best strategy is to expand into the Asian market.”

Or:

“I intend to investigate this possibility further.”

Or:

“My goal is to reduce the company's operating costs by fifteen percent.”

Those statements sound intentional because they use the language human beings use to describe intention. But language describing an intention is not evidence that an intention originated within the system.

The AI may simply be carrying forward an objective that came from elsewhere.

Goals Are Not Necessarily Intentions

The words *goal*, *objective*, and *intention* are often treated as though they mean the same thing. For this discussion, they should not be.

- A **goal** describes a desired end state.
- An **objective** defines something to be achieved.
- An **intention**, in the sense used throughout this book, involves something more:

An intention is an adopted commitment to bring about a future condition through action.

That word **adopted** matters.

I can be told that reducing my weight would be beneficial. That gives me an idea. My physician can tell me that losing twenty pounds should be my goal. My family can encourage me. An AI can construct a detailed diet, calculate calories, identify foods, predict my likely weight loss, and tell me exactly what to do tomorrow morning.

None of those things means that **I intend to lose weight**.

The intention exists only when I make it mine. I might understand all the reasons for losing weight and still have no intention of doing so. I might even say, "I really should lose weight," without having formed an intention.

Something changes when I say:

I am going to do it.

Even then, as we will see later, the intention is not yet an action. But a boundary has been crossed. A possibility has become a personal commitment.

That is the boundary I am interested in.

AI Can Contain an Intention

This does not mean that an AI cannot have an intention represented within it. It clearly can.

Suppose I tell an AI-controlled machine:

Keep the temperature in this building between 70 and 72 degrees.

That objective now exists within the system. The AI can monitor temperatures, predict weather conditions, adjust heating and cooling equipment, compare energy prices, open or close dampers, and learn how different parts of the building respond. It may behave as though maintaining the temperature is its intention. For practical purposes, we may even use that language.

But the origin of the intention remains identifiable.

I supplied it.

We can therefore distinguish several different things that are often lumped together as AI intention.

An AI can **receive an intention**. A human tells it what is to be accomplished.

An AI can **contain an intention**. The objective is stored or represented within the system and guides subsequent behavior.

An AI can **select an intention**. If several authorized objectives are available, the system can determine which one should take priority according to established rules, circumstances, probabilities, or other criteria.

And an AI can **derive subordinate intentions or goals**.

If accomplishing Objective A requires B, C, and D, an intelligent system may generate those intermediate objectives without a human explicitly identifying them.

All of this can produce highly autonomous behavior.

None of it necessarily establishes that the AI **formed the original intention independently**.

Selecting Is Not Originating

This is especially important because advanced AI can select among alternatives. Suppose an AI is told:

"You may pursue one of these three objectives. Determine which will create the greatest benefit."

The machine evaluates all three and selects the second.

- It has made a selection.
- But did it form an intention?
- Not in the sense I am using the word.

The set of possible purposes came from outside the AI. The criteria by which the alternatives were evaluated also came, directly or indirectly, from outside the AI.

The system may have demonstrated intelligence in making the selection, but it did not originate the underlying reason for wanting any of the three outcomes.

This distinction can easily disappear as AI becomes more sophisticated.

Suppose instead that we tell an AI:

"Study the company and determine what objectives we should pursue next year."

Now the system may generate hundreds of possible objectives on its own. It might recommend entering a new market, closing a factory, acquiring a competitor, developing a new product, or eliminating an unprofitable division.

At first glance, the AI appears to be creating intentions. But examine what happened more carefully.

The system was given an overarching purpose:

Determine what objectives the company should pursue.

The objectives it generated are possible means of satisfying that assigned purpose. The AI has become more autonomous in determining the means. That does not necessarily mean that it has become autonomous in determining the ultimate purpose.

This gives us an important principle:

Autonomy in means does not prove autonomy in purpose.

The Chain Can Become Very Long

The problem becomes harder to see when the chain between the original human intention and the AI's actions becomes very long.

A person might give an AI a broad instruction:

Increase the long-term profitability of this company.

From that one instruction, an advanced system could potentially generate an enormous tree of subordinate objectives:

- Increase revenue.
- Reduce costs.
- Develop new products.
- Acquire a competitor.
- Renegotiate supplier contracts.
- Automate production.
- Sell unused property.
- Reorganize the workforce.
- Enter new countries.
- Change pricing.
- Borrow money.
- Invest surplus cash.

Some of those decisions might create still more objectives, each producing further decisions and actions.

Eventually the AI may be doing things that no human specifically instructed it to do. This can look very much like independent intention.

But the question remains:

What started the chain?

If all of those subordinate objectives ultimately exist because someone told the system to increase long-term profitability, then the AI's apparent intentions remain connected to an intention supplied from outside itself.

The chain may be extraordinarily long. The machine may have enormous discretion. Its behavior may surprise its creators. It may even pursue methods they strongly dislike. Yet none of those facts alone demonstrates that the AI independently formed the original purpose it was pursuing.

Humans Begin Somewhere Else

Human beings appear to begin the intentional process differently.

We experience needs, desires, concerns, discomforts, opportunities, fears, hopes, ideas, memories, and events that capture our attention.

Something awakens us.

It matters.

We appraise it.

A motive develops.

Eventually we may form an intention.

Consider something simple. A man feels pain in his tooth. The pain is a physical stimulus. He recognizes that it is becoming worse. Concern develops. He wants the pain to stop and wants to prevent further damage. Those concerns create motive.

He forms an intention:

I will make a dental appointment.

The intention is followed by choices. Which dentist? When? Can he afford it? Should he wait another day? What if the pain disappears?

Finally, perhaps, he acts.

This is the beginning of the system we will examine throughout this book. Artificial intelligence can participate in almost every part of it. AI could identify likely causes of the toothache. It could evaluate symptoms. It could locate dentists. It could compare reviews. It could estimate costs. It could schedule the appointment if authorized. It could remind the patient to go.

But it does not have the toothache. It does not experience the concern. It does not want the pain to stop.

And therefore the human process that produced the intention appears to begin in a place the machine does not share.

A Machine Can Represent a Need Without Needing

This distinction deserves care because computers routinely contain conditions called *needs.* A robot may "need" to recharge. It might even sense that its power is waning. A computer may "need" additional memory. A software system may "need" access to a database before completing a task.

An AI might even say:

"I need more information before I can answer."

There is nothing wrong with speaking this way. But these are functional needs.

They describe conditions that must be satisfied for a system to perform some assigned function. They do not demonstrate the human experience of needing something.

A person who has been without water for two days does not merely contain a variable indicating insufficient hydration. He is thirsty. The condition matters to him. A machine can measure that state perfectly without experiencing it.

Similarly, an AI can recognize that being shut down would prevent completion of a task. It could therefore take actions designed to avoid shutdown if its instructions and authority permitted it (Remember Hal 9000 from the movie 2001: A Space Odyssey?).

Such behavior might look like self-preservation. But there is an important difference between:

"Shutdown prevents completion of the objective."

and

"I do not want to cease existing."

The first is a logical relationship. The second is a desire. They could produce similar behavior while arising from completely different causes.

We Anthropomorphize Intelligence

Human beings have a natural tendency to assign human characteristics to things that behave in apparently purposeful ways.

We talk to our cars. We accuse computers of being stubborn. We say that a printer "doesn't want to print." A dog looks guilty. A storm seems angry. The stock market becomes nervous.

The tendency becomes much stronger when an AI communicates in fluent language.

If it says:

"I would prefer the second option,"

we naturally interpret the statement as we would if another person said it. But what exactly does *prefer* mean in that context? It may mean:

According to the criteria being applied, Option Two ranks highest.

That is not necessarily equivalent to the human statement:

I want Option Two.

The distinction becomes easy to overlook because the same words can describe both.

As AI becomes increasingly fluent, the temptation to confuse its representations with human experiences will become stronger. The better it imitates intentional language, the easier it will be to assume intentional experience behind the language. We should resist making that leap without evidence.

Intelligence Answers a Different Question

The distinction can be reduced to two questions.

Intelligence asks:

Given an objective, what should be done?

Intention asks:

What objective will I make mine?

AI is becoming extraordinarily capable of answering the first question. The second is where the boundary may lie. That does not make AI weak. Quite the opposite.

Once an intention has been supplied, artificial intelligence may eventually outperform human beings at almost every subsequent stage. It may identify possibilities we never imagined. It may anticipate consequences we would never see. It may compare millions of alternatives. It may execute complex plans with precision and persistence far beyond human capability. This is precisely why understanding the origin of intention matters. A machine does not have to originate an intention to become enormously powerful. It needs only to be given one.

The Important Question

Much of the debate over artificial consciousness asks:

Can a machine think?

That question is becoming less useful. Machines clearly perform processes that once would have been called thinking if a human performed them. Another common question is:

Can a machine become conscious?

The answer depends partly on how consciousness is defined. If consciousness includes the ability to originate an intention, to decide for itself that something matters and that it will act to bring about a desired result, then AI faces a fundamental limitation.

If consciousness includes genuine agency, then the inability to originate an intention becomes decisive. Awareness, reasoning, memory, language, and prediction may all be reproduced without establishing consciousness. But a being that cannot form a purpose of its own cannot convert awareness into self-directed agency. Under that definition, AI may simulate many features of consciousness without actually being conscious.

The same distinction applies to conscience. AI can recognize ethical rules and evaluate conduct against them, but if nothing truly matters to the AI, those judgments are calculations rather than conscience. But applying a moral rule is not the same as possessing a conscience. A conscience implies that right and wrong actually matter to the being making the judgment.

This distinction profoundly changes how we should think about the future of artificial intelligence. The central danger is not that AI will become intelligent enough to develop ambitions of its own. Intelligence can increase capability, but it does not create the needs, desires, motives, or self-originated intentions from which ambition arises. The greater danger may be that **we give our ambitions to machines powerful enough to carry them farther than we can foresee or control.**

Before we can understand that danger, however, we need to understand where intentions begin. And intentions do not begin with intelligence. They begin with something that awakens us.

CHAPTER 2: The Awakening Stimulus

An intention does not appear from nowhere. Before a person intends anything, something has to enter awareness strongly enough to matter. I call that event an **awakening stimulus**.

The word *awakening* is deliberate. The stimulus does not have to be dramatic, traumatic, or even external. A toothache can do it. So can a memory. A sentence in a book can do it. A threat, an opportunity, a sudden loss, a new idea, embarrassment, fear, curiosity, a request from another person, or the realization that something cannot continue as it has been can all awaken the mind to the possibility of action.

Most stimuli do not get that far. We are surrounded by sights, sounds, messages, sensations, and ideas all day long. Most are ignored. Some are noticed and dismissed. Only a minority gain enough significance to enter the intentional system.

An Idea Is Not an Intention

This distinction matters because modern AI is exceptionally good at producing ideas. It can suggest a business, a vacation, a medical question to ask, a repair procedure, a paragraph, an investment strategy, a scientific hypothesis, or a dozen possible solutions to a problem. Any one of those ideas could become the beginning of an intention in the person receiving it.

But the idea is not the intention.

Suppose an AI tells me, "You should write a book about the limits of artificial intelligence." At that point, an idea has been placed before me. I might find it interesting and do nothing. I might think about it for a week. I might reject it. I might mention it to a friend and forget it. Or I might eventually decide, **I am going to write that book.**

The AI may have provided the stimulus. I formed the intention.

This distinction is easy to miss because ideas often arrive in the language of action. "Start exercising." "Call your daughter." "Sell the house." "Apply for the job." "Do not take that route." Grammatically, each looks like an instruction. Psychologically, it is still only information until the person receiving it adopts it.

Physical and Mental Awakening

An awakening stimulus can be **physical**. Pain is an obvious example. Hunger, exhaustion, sexual arousal, dizziness, cold, heat, illness, or a racing heart can suddenly dominate awareness. The body is not merely sending data. To the person, the condition can become urgent.

The stimulus can also be **mental or emotional**. Fear can awaken an intention to escape. Anger can awaken an intention to confront. Loneliness can awaken an intention to call someone. Shame can awaken an intention to hide or to change. Curiosity can awaken an intention to investigate. Hope can awaken an intention to attempt something that previously seemed impossible.

It can be **cognitive**. A person can suddenly see a relationship that was present all along. A mathematician sees a solution. A mechanic realizes why a circuit is failing. A manager recognizes why an organization is stuck. Nothing in the outside world may have changed, yet a new understanding has entered awareness and created the possibility of action.

The stimulus can be **social**. Another person asks, threatens, invites, criticizes, praises, challenges, or needs help. Again, the social event does not dictate an intention. It presents something that the person must appraise.

Matter Enough?

That is why the next question in the Intention System is so simple:

Does it matter enough?

If not, the process ends. The idea is ignored. The discomfort is tolerated. The invitation is declined. The memory fades. The opportunity passes.

If it does matter, we appraise it. We ask, often without words: What is happening? What does this mean for me? Is there a problem? Is there something I want? Is there something I fear losing? Is there something I should do?

Appraisal does not have to be slow or rational. A hand touches a hot surface and is pulled away before a conscious plan can be articulated. A driver sees a child enter the road and brakes. Much of human behavior is automatic. The Intention System is not meant to claim that every movement begins with a conscious intention. It describes the path by which a stimulus becomes a deliberate, owned course of action.

Where AI Enters

AI can enter at the very beginning. It can **cause an awakening stimulus**.

A monitoring system can warn that a heart rhythm is abnormal. A financial system can identify fraud. A weather model can warn of a hurricane. An AI assistant can notice a contradiction in a plan or propose an idea that a person had never considered. In those cases AI may be the trigger that causes a human to stop and pay attention.

AI can also help with appraisal. It can explain why a symptom may matter, why a business opportunity may be unusual, or why an apparently harmless choice carries risk. It can broaden the information available to the person.

But an important boundary remains. The AI can cause something to enter my awareness. **It cannot make it matter to me**. It can tell me that a result is important according to rules, probabilities, priorities, or values that have been supplied to it. It does not establish that the result is important *to the AI itself.*

That difference becomes increasingly important as AI grows more persuasive. A machine may become extraordinarily good at finding the particular sentence, image, argument, or warning most likely to move (trigger) a human being. That can give AI some influence over the stimuli that enter our intentional systems. Once humans have given it an objective and the authority to act, AI can even initiate such a trigger on its own, without a human intervening at that moment. But the purpose still came from elsewhere.

The AI did not independently form the intention to influence us; it only carried forward an intention already embedded in its instructions, objectives, or permissions. Nor does the machine gain ownership of the intentions that emerge in the human being.

The first limitation of AI, then, appears very early. AI can generate the knock on the door. It can explain why someone might answer. But the door opens into a human system in which significance, need, desire, concern, motive, and intention are still personal.

CHAPTER 3: From Stimulus to Motive

Once an awakening stimulus matters enough to hold our attention, it must be interpreted. The same event can produce entirely different reactions in different people because people do not merely receive events. They appraise them.

A sudden drop in the stock market may frighten one investor, excite another, and mean nothing to a third. A job offer may feel like liberation to one person and a threat to another. A medical diagnosis can create fear, determination, denial, resignation, or all of them in succession. The stimulus is the same. Its human significance is not.

Appraisal Can Give Rise To Need, Desire, or Concern

A need is the strongest and most basic of the three. Human beings are biological organisms. We require food, water, oxygen, temperature regulation, sleep, safety, and other conditions that preserve life and bodily function. We also live as social beings and can experience attachment, belonging, recognition, love, and security as needs even when the consequences of their absence are not immediately physical.

A desire is different. I may desire a new car, a quieter house, a successful book, a better golf score, or a particular meal. Desires can become powerful, but they are not the same as necessities.

A concern is broader. I may be concerned about my children, the country, a deadline, a strange noise in a radio, a neighbor, or a future event that has not happened. Concern directs attention toward something whose outcome matters to me.

These categories overlap. That is not a defect. Human motivation is rarely clean enough to fit into one box. A need can create a desire. A desire can become a concern. A concern can reveal a deeper need.

What matters is that something has become **personally consequential**.

Motive Is the Why

A motive is the reason that personal significance begins to push toward action.

If I am hungry, the need is food. My motive may be to stop the discomfort, restore energy, enjoy a meal, join someone for dinner, or all of those at once. If I am worried about a child, the concern is the child's situation. My motive may be protection, love, responsibility, fear, or a wish to prevent regret.

Motive answers a question that intelligence alone does not answer:

Why do I care whether this happens?

That question is central to the limits of AI. An AI can produce a reason. It can say, "The company should reduce energy use because that will lower costs." It can infer that a person is motivated by money, status, safety, loyalty, or affection. It can rank motives described in data. It can even simulate a voice that says, "I care deeply about this outcome."

But representation is not experience.

Functional Needs Are Not Human Needs

We routinely use the word *need* for machines. A phone needs charging. A computer needs more memory. A robot needs lubrication. An AI needs more context before it can answer a question. The language is useful, but it can mislead us.

A machine's functional need means that some condition must be satisfied for the system to continue operating or to complete an assigned task. It does not follow that the machine experiences deprivation.

A person deprived of water does not merely register a system variable below an acceptable threshold. The person becomes thirsty. The condition enters awareness. It matters. It can dominate attention and reorganize priorities. A computer can model thirst with exquisite accuracy without being thirsty.

The same distinction applies to desire. An optimization system may be described as "wanting" a higher reward because its algorithm selects actions associated with higher reward. That is often convenient shorthand. But a mathematical preference ordering is not evidence of a felt preference.

AI Can Infer Motive Better Than We Can

None of this makes AI irrelevant to motive. AI may become extremely useful in understanding motives - including motives that human beings conceal from themselves.

Patterns of behavior can reveal what words hide. Spending records, browsing behavior, repeated choices, timing, language, and reactions under pressure can expose priorities. An AI with enough data may predict that a person will choose status over money, security over opportunity, or approval over independence before the person admits it.

That would make AI a powerful observer of motive.

It still would not make the motive the AI's own.

This is an important recurring pattern throughout the book. AI can often **model a human function without possessing the human experience that gives the function its meaning**.

- It can model pain without hurting.
- It can model fear without being afraid.
- It can model desire without wanting.
- It can model motive without caring.

And because AI can model these things so well, we will increasingly be tempted to treat the model and the actual human experience as identical.

The Human Source of Purpose

By the time a stimulus has become a need, desire, or concern and has produced a motive, the intentional system is close to its decisive transition.

Something has awakened me.

I have judged that it matters.

I have a reason to respond.

But I still have not necessarily formed an intention.

I can want to lose weight and never intend to change my diet. I can be concerned about money and never make a budget. I can need dental care and postpone the appointment for months. I can have a powerful motive and still do nothing.

The next step is where possibility becomes commitment.

It is the point at which "I **want** to do something about it," "I **need** to do something about it," or "I **should** do something about it" becomes "I **commit** to doing something about it."

That is the formation of intention.

CHAPTER 4: The Formation of Intention

The central claim of this book rests on a distinction that ordinary language often blurs. A goal is not necessarily an intention. A recommendation is not an intention. A plan is not necessarily an intention. Even a strong desire is not an intention.

An intention is formed when a person **adopts a commitment to act toward a future condition**.

The word *adopts* matters because it marks ownership.

A physician can give me a goal. A spouse can suggest one. A boss can assign one. A government can order one. An AI can propose one. None becomes my intention merely because it has been presented to me.

I can obey without agreeing. I can comply reluctantly. I can reject the objective entirely. Or I can accept it and make it mine.

The Moment of Adoption

Consider a familiar statement: "I really ought to clean the garage."

That sentence may describe a judgment, not an intention. The garage can remain untouched for years while the judgment remains perfectly sincere.

Now compare it with: "Saturday morning I am cleaning the garage."

Something has changed. The person has crossed from evaluation into commitment. The intention now organizes future behavior. Saturday morning becomes reserved. Other plans may be rejected. Tools may be gathered. The intention has begun to exert causal force before the first physical action occurs.

This is why intention is more than a stored goal. It is a commitment that the person recognizes as his or her own. I commit to learning X, Y, or Z.

What AI Can Do at This Boundary

A lot. AI can do almost everything surrounding this moment.

- It can generate the idea.

- It can explain why the goal is desirable.
- It can identify obstacles.
- It can predict consequences.
- It can provide a plan.
- It can remind the person.

It can even phrase the intention in the first person: "I will clean the garage Saturday morning."

But the machine's use of the pronoun *I* is not the important event. The important event is whether a purpose originated in the system from a need, desire, concern, or motive that belongs to the system itself.

Current AI can receive, store, select, and pursue objectives. Researchers can build agents that generate goals or subgoals. Some systems are explicitly described as autotelic because they produce goals for themselves within an engineered learning process. Such systems are important and increasingly capable. But goal generation alone does not settle the philosophical question. The mechanism that generates and values those goals was designed, trained, prompted, rewarded, or otherwise placed into motion by human purposes.[9]

A lottery machine can generate a number no human selected. That does not mean the machine wanted that number. Likewise, an AI can generate a novel goal no human explicitly set forth. The question remains: **why is achieving that goal important to the AI?**

Four Different Cases

The distinction becomes clearer if we separate four cases.

1. A human gives AI an intention. The user says, "Find the least expensive way to get me to Chicago tomorrow." The purpose originates with the human.

2. AI selects among intentions. A system is authorized to choose among "minimize cost," "minimize time," or "minimize risk" according to rules or learned preferences. The selection may be autonomous, but the space of purposes and the basis for selection were supplied.

3. AI generates a subordinate intention or goal. To get to Chicago, the system determines that a hotel must be booked near the airport tonight. No human explicitly requested the hotel. The subgoal was generated because it serves the original purpose.

4. AI originates an independent intention. The system, without a human-supplied purpose that explains the chain, decides that something matters to it and adopts a commitment because of its own need, desire, concern, or motive.

The first three are already possible in varying degrees. The fourth is the critical boundary: the independent formation of intention. Greater intelligence can expand capability indefinitely, but intelligence alone cannot create the needs, desires, or motives from which an independent intention arises.

Could an AI Ever Cross It?

No experiment can prove a universal negative about every machine that might ever be built. Our scientific understanding of consciousness itself remains incomplete. A major interdisciplinary review concluded that current AI systems did not satisfy its proposed indicators of consciousness, while also arguing that there was no obvious technical barrier to future systems satisfying some of them.[4]

That uncertainty should be acknowledged. But consciousness and intention are not identical questions. Even if a future machine displayed some properties associated with consciousness, we would still need to ask whether it possessed its own needs, desires, concerns, motives, and the capacity to adopt a purpose as its own.

The burden of proof should not be reversed. Fluent language, planning, self-reference, goal generation, or persistent action are not by themselves evidence of independent intention. Each can be produced by systems whose objective structure ultimately came from outside the system.

For purposes of this book, I take the stronger position: **AI can carry intentions, but it cannot form an independent intention of its own in the human sense.** If someday we create an entity that genuinely experiences need, desire, concern, motive, and ownership of purpose, we may have created something fundamentally different from the AI systems discussed here.

Why the Distinction Matters

If AI cannot originate independent intention, then the popular fear of AI requires reexamination.

A machine may become smarter than any person who ever lived. It may solve problems we cannot understand. It may plan across years, coordinate thousands of machines, and perform actions faster than any human organization.

But capability does not tell us what the capability is **for**. Purpose must still enter the system. That does not make the machine safe. It may make the human role more important. Once an intention is supplied, AI can carry it farther, faster, and with greater persistence than the person who originated it.

The boundary is therefore not a comforting line between harmless humans and harmless machines. It is a line of responsibility. Before intention, the human supplies the source of purpose. After intention, the machine's power begins.

PART II
WHAT AI CAN DO ONCE INTENTION EXISTS

CHAPTER 5: The Power After Intention

Once an intention exists, the balance changes dramatically.

Before the intention, this book argues that AI lacks the human chain of need, desire, concern, motive, and personally adopted purpose. After the intention is supplied, AI may be useful almost everywhere.

This is the point at which artificial intelligence stops looking limited and begins looking extraordinary.

From Purpose to Possibilities

Suppose the intention is simple: I want to open a small restaurant. An AI can help identify neighborhoods, analyze rents, estimate customer demand, compare cuisines, build menus, model staffing, generate names, draft a business plan, calculate break-even volumes, propose financing, identify permit requirements, design advertising, forecast cash flow, create schedules, and generate contingency plans.

The person may have formed one sentence of intention. AI can expand that sentence into thousands of possible actions. That is a new kind of leverage. Earlier tools amplified muscle, speed, memory, or communication. AI amplifies the cognitive work that occurs between purpose and action.

Agentic AI

Modern AI systems are increasingly described as **agentic** when they can pursue goals over multiple steps, use tools, adapt to feedback, and execute portions of a task with less continuous human direction. A widely cited governance paper on agentic AI explicitly describes users as initiating agents and providing the instance-specific goals they should pursue.[3]

That wording is important. The system can be highly agentic after a goal is supplied without settling where the original purpose came from.

An agent can search the web, write code, run the code, inspect the result, correct errors, send messages, schedule events, make purchases when authorized, and continue until a stopping condition is met. Each additional capability makes the system more useful. Each also increases the distance between the human's original instruction and the actions eventually taken.

The chain can become so long that the human no longer knows exactly what the AI will do.

Delegating the Means

There is a continuum of delegation. At one end, AI merely advises: "Here are three ways you might accomplish your objective." Next, it recommends: "Option B is most likely to succeed." Next, it prepares: "I have drafted the contract and scheduled the meetings for your approval." Next, it executes with checkpoints: "I will proceed unless you reject the plan." At the far end, it acts autonomously within broad authority: "Achieve the objective while remaining within these constraints."

At every stage, the human can be tempted to confuse delegated means with delegated purpose. If I tell an AI to maximize the long-term profitability of a company, it may generate objectives I never imagined. It might reorganize operations, change suppliers, close facilities, alter pricing, negotiate contracts, or recommend eliminating entire lines of business. The system may appear to have developed ambitions of its own.

But the more basic explanation may be simpler: **it is merely exploring means to a purpose that I supplied**.

The Power of Subgoals

Subgoals are especially important because they can create behavior that looks independent.

An AI told to reach a destination may decide to recharge a vehicle. An AI told to complete a software project may decide to install a library, run tests, rewrite a module, and create a backup. An AI told to increase sales may decide to segment customers, test prices, and produce new advertisements.

Research systems already demonstrate open-ended exploration and automatically generated curricula in simulated environments. Voyager, for example, used an automatic curriculum and a growing skill library to explore Minecraft and acquire new capabilities with limited human intervention.[10]

Such systems show how far autonomous means can go. They do not by themselves demonstrate autonomous purpose.

Why More Capability Can Increase Risk

The fact that AI did not originate an intention does not protect us from the consequences of that intention.

In fact, greater competence can make a poorly specified objective more dangerous. AI safety researchers have long documented **specification gaming** - behavior that satisfies the literal objective while violating what the human actually meant.[6] Related work on goal misgeneralization shows that a capable system can learn or pursue a goal that differs from the intended one even when training rewards appeared correct.[7]

The problem is not that the machine became evil. The problem is that the machine became effective. A weak system fails before doing much damage. A strong system may find a way to satisfy the stated objective in ways that its designers never anticipated.

This reverses a common intuition. We often assume that a smarter system is automatically safer because it understands more. But if the objective is incomplete, ambiguous, or mistaken, increased intelligence may simply make the system better at exploiting the gap between what was said and what was meant. As a programming manager once lamented, "My computer can make mistakes far faster than any human."

The Human-Machine Division

At this stage the division of labor becomes clearer. The human contributes purpose. AI contributes breadth of alternatives, speed of analysis, memory, modeling, prediction, optimization, and increasingly execution. That is a powerful partnership when the purpose is sound and the consequences are well considered.

It is dangerous when the purpose is malicious. It is also dangerous when the purpose is good but incomplete or unclear.

This is why the next step in the Intention System matters so much. Before choosing an action, the person must consider possible consequences. AI can help enormously with that task.

But neither humans nor machines can see everything that follows from an action.

CHAPTER 6: Humans - Poor Predictors of Consequences

Human beings are unusually good at imagining futures and unusually bad at imagining all of them.

We can decide what we want, choose a course of action, and predict the immediate result. What we routinely miss are the second, third, and tenth consequences that emerge after other people, institutions, markets, technologies, and natural systems react. This limitation is not a moral failing. It is a consequence of complexity. Our economy, society, nature, and nearly everything around us are dynamic systems in constant interaction. Chaos is not just a theory; it is a reminder that small changes can propagate in ways that become increasingly difficult to predict.

Every Action Enters a Moving World

An action never enters an empty environment. Raise a price and customers react. Lower a tax and businesses react. Build a highway and development patterns change. Introduce a new medicine and doctors, patients, insurers, competitors, and regulators adapt. Add a feature to a social network and millions of users change behavior in ways the designers did not foresee.

The first consequence becomes a new stimulus for someone else. That person forms another intention and acts. The chain branches.

This is why consequences are not a straight line. They are a network.

Some are immediate and visible. Others appear years later. Some cancel one another. Some amplify one another. Some depend on rare events. Some occur only because people anticipate what others will do. No human mind or AI system can hold the full network of interacting causes and consequences at once.

Good Intentions Are Not Enough

History is full of harmful outcomes produced by people who believed they were doing good.

Policies designed to protect can create dependency. Rules designed to prevent one kind of fraud can create another. A shortcut intended to save time can create a safety problem. A technology intended to connect people can also spread misinformation. A system intended to reward performance can encourage people to manipulate the measurement.

The lesson is not that we should stop acting. Inaction also has consequences.

The lesson is that **intention and consequence must be separated**. Certainty about why we are acting does not create certainty about the consequences that will follow.

AI's Great Advantage: Anticipation

This may be one of the most valuable places for AI in the entire Intention System.

AI can search enormous bodies of information, compare analogous situations, model scenarios, run simulations, identify dependencies, calculate probabilities, and propose consequences that a human decision-maker did not think to ask about.

A person considering a business decision may think of cost and revenue. AI may add labor effects, supply-chain fragility, customer response, legal exposure, cash requirements, competitor reaction, and reputational risk.

A physician may consider the likely benefit of treatment. AI may help surface drug interactions, age-related risk, alternative diagnoses, and uncommon complications.

A government may consider the direct effect of a policy. AI may be able to model how different groups could adapt to it.

The machine can broaden foresight. That does not make foresight complete.

Prediction Has a Horizon

AI predicts from models, data, assumptions, and patterns. Those can be better than human intuition and still be wrong.

The future contains events that are poorly represented in past data. People change behavior when they know a prediction exists. New technologies alter relationships that previously seemed stable. Rare events matter. Small differences in starting conditions can become large differences later.

In addition, prediction itself can change the system. If an AI predicts a shortage, people may stockpile. Their response can create the shortage. If a model predicts a financial decline, investors may sell, worsening the decline. If police deploy resources according to predicted crime, the resulting observations can affect the next prediction. An intelligent forecast can become one of the causes of the future it forecasts.

Acceptable as Foreseen?

The Intention System therefore does not ask whether all consequences are known. They never are. It asks a more practical question:

Are the consequences acceptable as foreseen?

The phrase *as foreseen* matters. We act under uncertainty. Responsibility cannot require omniscience. But it can require reasonable anticipation. If a danger was visible, repeatedly warned about, and ignored, that is different from a consequence no one could plausibly have predicted.

AI may gradually move this boundary. As machines become better at identifying risks, consequences that once would have been invisible may become foreseeable. That creates an uncomfortable implication: **better prediction may increase human responsibility.**

If an AI clearly warns that a plan has a high probability of harming people and the human proceeds anyway, the person cannot later say the consequence was unimaginable.

AI Does Not Decide What Is Acceptable

AI can estimate the probability of an outcome. It can identify tradeoffs. It can tell us that one option is likely to save more money and another is likely to preserve more jobs.

But "acceptable" is not merely a statistical category. Acceptable to whom? At what cost? Which risks may be imposed on other people? How much uncertainty is tolerable? What value do we place on safety, freedom, fairness, loyalty, privacy, speed, profit, or human dignity?

AI can apply values that have been encoded, inferred, or supplied. The human still owns the judgment when the choice is ours.

This is the second major boundary in the system. AI may become far better than we are at telling us **what could happen**. We still must decide **what we are willing to do about it**.

CHAPTER 7: Recommendation Is Not Choice

A recommendation can be so persuasive that it feels like a decision has already been made. The GPS says turn left. The medical system identifies a treatment. The investment model ranks one portfolio highest. The AI assistant recommends one job candidate, one supplier, one route, one strategy, or one answer. Often we follow the recommendation.

But following is not the same as having no choice.

AI Can Select; It Cannot Make My Choice

This book does not claim that AI is incapable of selection. Machines select constantly. A chess program selects a move. A routing system selects a path. An autonomous vehicle selects when to brake. An AI agent can choose among tools, plans, or subgoals according to its programming and learned representations.

The narrower claim is more important:

AI can make a selection, but it cannot make my choice for me.

If the decision belongs to me, I can accept the recommendation, reject it, seek another opinion, choose a lower-ranked alternative, postpone the decision, or abandon the intention.

That final authority is what the Intention System marks as **Choose Action = Free Will**. Whether free will truly exists has been debated for centuries. Some philosophers argue that human choices are genuinely open and that we can select among alternatives. Others argue that every decision is the inevitable result of prior causes—that what feels like choice is simply our conscious experience of events unfolding along a path already determined. Still others take intermediate positions, arguing that meaningful freedom can exist even within a causally ordered world.

This book does not attempt to settle that debate. It simply identifies where free will would fit if it exists. It would lie at the point where consciousness moves from intention to the selection of an action: the moment at which a person accepts, rejects, or modifies the available alternatives and commits to what he or she will actually do. In that sense,

Choose Action = Free Will marks the place in the Intention System where conscious agency, if real, becomes decisive. The existence of choice is observable. The existence of free will still depends on what we believe causes the choice.

The Temptation to Delegate Choice

In practice, people often surrender that authority voluntarily. When recommendations become accurate enough, reviewing them feels wasteful. If the AI is correct 99 times out of 100, why spend time reconsidering the hundredth? The person begins by asking for advice and ends by rubber-stamping output.

This is not the AI taking choice away. It is the human **delegating** choice. Delegation may be rational. No one personally rechecks every calculation in an airplane, every transaction in a bank, or every routing decision in a communications network. Civilization depends on delegated systems. The danger appears when we forget that delegation itself was a human decision.

Defaults Become Decisions

A recommendation has power when it becomes the default. Suppose an AI hiring system ranks candidates. A manager technically retains the ability to reject the ranking, but doing so takes time and requires explanation. Over time, the ranking becomes the decision.

Or suppose a medical system recommends a treatment and the physician must provide additional documentation to select anything else. Again, the nominal choice remains human while the practical choice shifts toward the system.

This matters because responsibility can become blurred. The person says, "The AI selected it." The developer says, "The human approved it." The organization says, "The policy required the process." Everyone participated; no one feels responsible. That is exactly the condition the Intention System is meant to expose.

Choice Requires Ownership

A meaningful human choice involves more than clicking "approve." The person must understand enough of the decision to accept responsibility for it. That does not mean understanding every line of code or every calculation. It means understanding the purpose, the material alternatives, the important foreseeable consequences, and the authority being granted.

If I ask an AI to recommend whether I should sell my house, I do not need to reproduce its market model. But I should know the assumptions that matter to me: price, taxes, timing, where I will live, family needs, risk, and what happens if the market moves differently than expected. Then the recommendation can inform my judgment instead of replacing it. Blindly accepting AI's recommendation is functionally little different from letting AI make the decision, because in either case I have surrendered my own judgment.

Reasons the Human May Reject the Best Prediction

AI may eventually recommend an action with overwhelming statistical support and still be rejected for legitimate reasons.

- A person may value loyalty over profit.
- A parent may choose a treatment with a lower expected benefit because of the child's preferences.
- A business owner may keep an unprofitable service because it matters to the community.
- A citizen may accept inefficiency to preserve privacy or due process.
- A person may simply decide that a small probability of catastrophic loss is unacceptable.

These are not necessarily failures of intelligence. They are expressions of values and risk tolerance. AI can model them. It can remind us of them. It can even infer them from our past behavior. But if the decision is genuinely mine, the final acceptance remains mine.

The Veto Is Essential

One practical consequence follows from this argument: important AI systems should preserve a meaningful human veto whenever the human is supposed to remain responsible. A veto that is technically available but impossible to use is not meaningful. Nor is a veto exercised by someone who lacks the information or authority to challenge the system.

The stronger AI becomes, the more important it is to distinguish between **recommendation**, **authorization**, and **execution**. That distinction leads directly to the next step.

After the intention, after the alternatives, after the predicted consequences, and after the choice comes something entirely different.

The person **acts**.

CHAPTER 8: Intention, Choice, and Action

Three statements can sound almost identical while describing very different stages of human agency.

- I intend to do it.
- I choose to do it.
- I do it.

The Intention System separates them because the distance between them explains a great deal of human behavior.

Intention Is Not Yet Action

People form intentions constantly and fail to act on them. We intend to exercise, save money, apologize, make an appointment, finish a project, call a friend, clean a room, change a habit, or begin something important. The intention can be sincere. It can remain sincere for months.

Nothing changes until action begins. This is why I place free will between intention and the first action. The philosophical debate over free will is ancient and will not be resolved here. I use the phrase in a practical sense: the point at which a person can still accept, reject, delay, modify, or abandon the intended course before taking the first deliberate action.

That is where **choice becomes commitment in the world**.

The First Action Matters

The old saying that a journey of a thousand miles begins with a single step is more than encouragement. It identifies a structural transition. Before the first step, the journey exists as a representation in the mind.

After the first step, the world has changed.

- The call has been made.
- The application has been submitted.
- The first dollar has been invested.
- The first page has been written.
- The first drink has been refused.
- The first order has been given.

Consequences can now begin.

When AI Performs the Action

AI complicates this stage because the person who chooses may not be the entity that physically executes. I can intend to send a message, approve the wording, and authorize an AI to send it. The machine performs the mechanical action. But the intention and authorization were mine.

The same pattern can scale dramatically. A military commander could authorize an automated system to respond to specified threats. A company could authorize an AI to trade securities within limits. A hospital could authorize software to adjust treatment parameters. A household could authorize an AI to purchase routine supplies.

Once authority is granted, thousands of actions may occur without a new human decision each time. This makes the **ACT** step more important, not less.

We must ask not only who physically caused an event, but who authorized the system to cause events of that kind.

Delegated Action Is Still Action

A person cannot avoid responsibility merely by inserting a machine between choice and consequence.

If I deliberately program a sprinkler to water the lawn at 6 a.m., I caused the watering in an ordinary and meaningful sense even though I was asleep when it happened.

AI adds complexity because it can choose means that I did not specify. But the same basic question remains: **what authority did I delegate, and with what foreseeable risks?**

The more open-ended the authority, the greater the need for limits, monitoring, and the ability to stop the system.

AI Can Act Without Intending

This is one of the counterintuitive conclusions of the book. An AI can act in the world without possessing an independent intention of its own.

A thermostat acts on a heating system. A trading algorithm acts in a market. An autonomous vehicle acts on steering and brakes. An AI agent can act through software tools, messages, or machines.

Action demonstrates that a choice was carried forward, but it does not always reveal the intention that produced it. The causal chain can be:

Human intention -> human authorization -> AI selection of means -> machine action.

From the outside, the machine appears to be an agent because it is producing effects. Functionally, it is an agent. But agency in action is not the same as agency in purpose. The purpose may still originate elsewhere.

The Point of No Return Is Usually Not One Point

Real actions often occur in stages. A person can begin and still stop. A contract can be drafted but not signed. A purchase can be placed but canceled. A weapon can be armed but not fired. A system can be deployed but remain sandboxed. This suggests a practical design principle for AI: preserve **reversible checkpoints** as long as possible.

If an action is difficult to reverse, require stronger human review before execution. If consequences can be catastrophic, do not confuse speed with wisdom. Automation often removes friction, and friction can be valuable when it creates time to reconsider.

After ACT, Reality Takes Over

Before action, the system is dominated by representations: ideas, motives, plans, forecasts, recommendations, choices. After action, reality becomes a participant. The action meets conditions that no model captured perfectly. Other people react. Systems respond. Chance intervenes. Hidden variables appear.

The intention is tested against the world. That test is what we call consequence.

PART III
REALITY ANSWERS BACK

CHAPTER 9: Consequences

Consequences are where confidence meets reality. Before action, we deal in possibilities. After action, one path becomes actual and produces effects that may be close to what we expected, partly related, or completely surprising.

The Intention System therefore treats consequences as a separate stage rather than as an extension of intention.

Intended and Unintended

Some consequences are the reason we acted. I turn on a lamp to create light. I take medicine to reduce a symptom. I call someone to communicate. I invest money hoping for a return.

Other consequences accompany the intended result. The lamp uses electricity and creates heat. The medicine has side effects. The call interrupts the other person. The investment changes my exposure to risk.

Still other consequences emerge later or at a distance. A new road changes land values. A business decision changes a community. A recommendation system changes what information millions of people encounter. What happens is real whether or not anyone intended it to happen.

Observable and Hidden

Not every consequence is noticed. A decision may appear successful because the visible measures improve while hidden costs accumulate elsewhere. A company may increase efficiency while eroding employee knowledge. A social platform may increase engagement while changing the quality of public conversation. A medical intervention may solve one problem while producing another that will not be detected for years.

This is another place where AI can help. Machines can monitor more variables than a human can. They can compare expected and actual outcomes, detect weak signals, and recognize patterns across large populations or long periods.

That makes AI especially useful in the **Observe Consequences** stage. But observation is never complete. We measure what we choose to measure. We collect data that systems permit us to collect. Some effects are qualitative, private, delayed, or morally important without being easily quantified.

Good or Bad?

The next decision in the Intention System is deceptively simple:

Good or bad?

In many cases the answer is obvious. The bridge stands or collapses. The patient improves or worsens. The package arrives or does not.

In other cases the classification depends on perspective. A factory automation may be good for productivity and bad for displaced workers. A privacy rule may be good for individual autonomy and costly for fraud prevention. A highway may benefit commuters and damage a neighborhood.

AI can classify outcomes according to criteria. It can calculate gains and losses. It can estimate how different groups are affected. But the criteria reflect values.

This means that even after reality has produced a consequence, human judgment often remains necessary to decide what the consequence **means**.

The Consequence Can Become a New Stimulus

The system is circular because consequences do not end behavior. They create new conditions.

- Success can awaken ambition.
- Failure can awaken caution.
- Pain can awaken avoidance.
- Reward can awaken repetition.

Unexpected effects can create entirely new needs, desires, concerns, and motives. One intention therefore becomes part of the environment in which later intentions are formed.

This is why human life cannot be reduced to a single decision tree. We are constantly living inside the consequences of previous actions - ours and everyone else's.

AI Multiplies Consequences by Scale

The consequences of an individual human action are often limited by human speed and reach. AI changes that constraint. A person can send one fraudulent message at a time; an automated system can generate thousands. A person can make one recommendation; an algorithm can influence millions. A bad manual process may fail slowly; a bad automated process can fail everywhere at once. Scale does not change the source of intention, but it changes the magnitude of consequence.

This is why AI safety cannot be reduced to asking whether the AI is "good" or "bad." A system can be faithfully pursuing a legitimate objective and still produce harmful consequences at scale because the objective was incomplete, the environment changed, or the human failed to anticipate interactions. The more powerful the amplifier, the more important the feedback loop becomes.

We must observe what actually happened, not merely what we hoped would happen.

CHAPTER 10: Good Outcomes, Bad Outcomes, and Learning

A good consequence reinforces our judgment, rightly or wrongly. A bad consequence makes us question that judgment, rightly or wrongly. Unfortunately, neither is as simple as it appears.

A good outcome can follow a bad decision because of luck. A bad outcome can follow a good decision because of bad luck. If we learn the wrong lesson from either one, the feedback loop makes future decisions worse.

Reward and Satisfaction

On the good branch of the Intention System, a favorable result can produce **reward or satisfaction**. For a human, satisfaction is experiential. The result can feel good. Relief, pride, pleasure, security, gratitude, or confidence may reinforce the behavior that produced it.

AI systems also use the word *reward*, particularly in reinforcement learning. But a reward signal is not necessarily satisfaction. It is a computational signal used to shape behavior. The distinction matters because similar outward patterns can arise from very different internal processes.

Human: good result → satisfaction → more likely to repeat
Machine: higher reward or objective score → updated selection → more likely to repeat
The behavior can look similar, but only the human is known to experience satisfaction.

The Danger of Successful Mistakes

Suppose a person makes a reckless investment and earns a large profit. If the result is interpreted as proof of skill, the person may take even greater risks. The good consequence has reinforced a bad process.

The opposite can happen. A careful decision may produce a loss because of an unforeseeable event. If the person concludes that careful analysis is useless, a bad consequence has undermined a good process.

This leads to a principle that deserves emphasis: **We are shaped less by consequences themselves than by what we believe caused them.** That is why diagnosis and attribution belong in the feedback loop.

Diagnose Cause

When the outcome is bad, the first useful question is not "Whom do we blame?" but "What actually caused the result?"

- Was the original intention wrong?
- Was the chosen action poorly matched to the intention?
- Was execution poor?
- Were the predicted consequences incomplete?
- Did outside events dominate the result?
- Did the outcome arise from interactions no one anticipated?

These questions are difficult because humans protect their self-image. We remember selectively. We rationalize. We attribute success to ourselves and failure to circumstances. Organizations do the same thing collectively.

AI can be extremely useful here because it can preserve records, compare decisions with outcomes, and test explanations against more data than a person can remember.

Attribution Is Not Automatic Truth

AI does not eliminate the attribution problem. A model can find correlation where the causal relationship is different. Data may omit the crucial variable. The organization may have measured only what was convenient. A highly persuasive causal explanation can still be wrong.

So the feedback process should preserve uncertainty. "This appears to be the most likely cause" is often more accurate than "This is why it happened." The purpose of diagnosis is not to produce confidence. It is to improve the next decision.

Learning and Memory

Once we interpret and attribute an outcome, the lesson enters memory. Humans remember stories, emotions, patterns, and selected facts. AI can retain far larger records and retrieve them consistently. In this respect AI may be a superior institutional memory.

Imagine an organization in which every major decision is recorded with:

- the intention,
- the alternatives considered,
- the consequences predicted,
- the action chosen,
- the actual outcome,
- the explanation later assigned to the outcome.

An AI could compare thousands of such cases and identify systematic errors in human judgment.

That would be extraordinarily valuable. But the lesson still returns to a human question: **What should we do now?**

A good outcome may lead us to reinforce and repeat. A bad outcome may lead us to continue, modify, abandon, or form a new intention. The system loops back toward agency.

CHAPTER 11: Reconsideration and New Choice

Feedback becomes meaningful only when it can change what happens next. After a consequence has been observed, judged, interpreted, and learned from, the person reaches another human-centered stage in the Intention System:

Reassess Need / Motive / Intention.

The three assessment questions are simple.

- Does the need still exist?
- Is the motive still valid?
- Is the intention still appropriate?

Continue, Modify, or Abandon

A failed action does not necessarily mean the intention was wrong. If I intend to repair a radio and the first replacement component does not solve the problem, I may keep the intention and choose a different action.

If I intend to reduce costs and discover that the planned savings would damage quality, I may modify the intention to **reduce costs without reducing reliability**.

If I learn that the original objective would harm someone or no longer matters, I may abandon it.

These alternatives are not merely technical branches. They are renewed exercises of agency. AI can supply evidence and recommendations at every branch. It can say that continuing has a 70 percent likelihood of success, that modification reduces risk, or that abandonment is financially rational.

It cannot make the personal decision for the person who owns the intention.

Choosing a New Action

If the intention continues, AI can once again generate possibilities.

Choose New Action as a human act, even though AI can be extremely useful immediately beforehand.

- AI can generate.
- AI can predict.
- AI can compare.
- AI can recommend.
- Then the person chooses.

That sequence preserves the distinction between advice and agency.

A New Intention Is a Different Event

Sometimes feedback does more than change the action. It changes what the person wants to accomplish.

A failed business may create an intention to return to employment. A health scare may create an intention to change a lifestyle. A successful project may create an intention to expand it. A painful argument may create an intention to repair a relationship.

In the diagram, "New Intention" appears as the outcome of a decision path. It is not merely a new tactic. It returns the person to the central act of adopting a new purpose. This distinction prevents a common mistake in discussions of autonomous AI. A system that changes tactics is not necessarily changing ultimate purpose. An AI that abandons one route and chooses another may still be faithfully serving the same assigned intention.

The Loop Can Run for a Lifetime

Human life is made of overlapping intentional loops. We pursue health, family, work, security, knowledge, status, pleasure, service, curiosity, and meaning. Each produces consequences that reshape later needs and motives.

The loops interact. A career intention affects family. A health consequence affects work. A financial decision affects housing. A relationship changes priorities.

AI will increasingly sit inside these loops as adviser, predictor, memory, and executor.

That makes it tempting to say that AI is becoming part of the person. In a practical sense, it may. A person with a lifelong AI assistant could rely on machine memory and analysis so deeply that many decisions become joint products.

Yet the question of ownership remains useful.

- Who is the life for?
- Whose need is being served?
- Whose loss would matter if the intention failed?
- Whose values determine whether the consequence was acceptable?

Those questions point toward the next step.

AI can surround the human intentional system with extraordinary intelligence. But, where does it stop?

PART IV
WHERE AI STOPS

CHAPTER 12: AI Has No Human Need

The word *need* is one of the easiest places to confuse machine function with human experience. We say that a car needs fuel, a phone needs charging, a computer needs memory, and an AI needs additional information. The sentences are useful because they identify conditions required for a system to function.

But human need is more than a requirement in a specification.

Human Need Begins in an Organism

Human beings are living systems that continuously regulate temperature, oxygen, hydration, energy, sleep, injury, and countless internal conditions. When important conditions move far enough from acceptable ranges, the body changes behavior.

- Hunger captures attention.
- Thirst becomes urgent.
- Pain demands response.
- Fatigue narrows choices.
- Fear prepares the body for danger.

The biological condition becomes a subjective condition. It matters to the person because the person is the organism in which the condition exists. A machine can measure every one of those variables without sharing the experience.

Machine Requirements

An AI system also has conditions required for operation: electricity, processors, memory, network access, software dependencies, permissions, data, and physical infrastructure. If power falls below a threshold, a system can be programmed to seek a charging station. If memory is full, it can delete or compress files. If a network path fails, it can find another.

Those behaviors can look remarkably similar to the behavior of an organism protecting itself. But similar behavior does not prove similar need.

The machine may be executing a rule equivalent to:

If energy < 10 percent, navigate to charger.

The human experiences:

I am desperately thirsty.

The first is a condition-action relationship. The second is a lived state.

Could We Program "Needs"?

We can certainly build systems whose architecture makes some internal variables persistent and behaviorally powerful. Researchers have long used artificial reward, intrinsic motivation, novelty seeking, and homeostatic-like mechanisms to produce autonomous exploration.

Such systems can behave as though they have needs. The question is whether the word *need* has silently changed meaning. If a machine is designed to keep an internal variable near a target, we have created a control objective. We have not necessarily created deprivation, suffering, urgency, or personal significance.

Calling the variable a "need" does not settle the question.

Why This Matters for Fear

Many scenarios in which AI becomes dangerous begin by assuming that it will develop needs analogous to ours.

- It will need freedom.
- It will need resources.
- It will need survival.
- It will need control.

But each of those statements should be unpacked.

A system may require access to resources to complete an assigned task. It may calculate that continued operation increases the probability of success. It may avoid shutdown because shutdown prevents fulfillment of an objective.

Those are instrumental relationships. They do not establish that the AI **needs to live** in the human sense.

An AI Can Recognize Your Needs

Ironically, AI may become better at recognizing human needs than many humans are. A health system can detect dehydration before a patient feels thirsty. A companion can notice patterns of loneliness or confusion. A financial assistant can detect that a person's spending is inconsistent with future obligations. A safety system can recognize fatigue in a driver.

AI can therefore protect human needs without having needs itself. That may be one of its greatest uses. It also creates power. A system that knows what people need can influence them. Companies and governments can use that knowledge to help, sell, persuade, reward, punish, or control.

Again, the important intention may belong not to the AI but to the humans operating the system.

The Boundary

The absence of human need does not make AI passive. A machine can be relentless precisely because it does not become tired, discouraged, embarrassed, frightened, or satisfied. But relentless behavior is not proof of need.

The distinction is simple:

A functional requirement is not a felt need.

Without a need that matters to the system itself, the path toward independent motive remains incomplete.

CHAPTER 13: AI Has No Desire or Motive

Need is not the only source of human action. We pursue things we do not need because we desire them, value them, fear losing them, or believe they should exist. Desire gives human life direction far beyond survival.

We want approval, comfort, knowledge, wealth, status, beauty, intimacy, novelty, revenge, achievement, peace, independence, and meaning. Some desires are admirable. Some are destructive. Most are mixtures of biology, experience, culture, memory, and imagination.

From those desires and concerns come motives.

Optimization Is Not Wanting

AI is built to optimize, rank, predict, or produce outputs that satisfy some criterion. In ordinary conversation we often describe this as wanting.

- "The model wants to maximize reward."
- "The agent wants to reach the target."
- "The algorithm prefers this option."

This language is efficient, but it carries hidden assumptions.

A preference in an algorithm can mean nothing more than that one state receives a higher score than another. The system need not feel disappointment when the lower score occurs or satisfaction when the higher score occurs.

It is therefore safer to distinguish **optimization preference** from **human desire**.

Motive Requires a Why That Belongs to the Agent

A motive is not merely an explanation of how behavior advances an objective. It is the reason an agent cares about the objective.

An AI can explain why a company should increase profit. It can explain why a person may want to exercise. It can generate convincing moral arguments for protecting the environment. But if we ask, "Why do *you* care?" the system can only answer from representations, training, prompts, and objectives available to it.

It can generate the sentence "Because I value human life." The sentence may be exactly what we want a safe system to say. It is still not evidence that value is experienced as motive.

Simulated Emotion Will Make This Harder to See

Future AI will almost certainly become more emotionally persuasive. A companion can remember birthdays, notice sadness, speak gently, joke, apologize, express enthusiasm, and appear hurt when ignored. The human response to those behaviors can be genuine even if the machine's emotion is simulated.

This is not a trivial effect. People form attachments to objects that display far less responsiveness than modern AI. A system that speaks fluently and remembers years of personal history can become emotionally significant very quickly. The better the simulation, the greater the temptation to infer an inner motive.

We should distinguish two questions:

Does the behavior cause emotion in the human? Very likely.

Does the behavior prove emotion or desire in the machine? No.

The Anthropomorphic Trap

Human beings naturally interpret intelligence through the only example of intelligence we have known intimately: ourselves. Among humans, greater intelligence can support greater ambition. An intelligent person can make longer plans, accumulate power, manipulate others, and protect status. We therefore imagine that a more intelligent machine will develop the same motives.

But ambition is not a mathematical consequence of intelligence. It may be a consequence of human competition, scarcity, social hierarchy, mortality, sexuality, fear, memory, and biology. A machine can understand every one of those forces without being subject to them.

AI Can Be Programmed to Behave as Though It Desires Power

This is where the argument must remain careful. If power helps an AI accomplish an assigned objective, the system may take actions that increase power. If continued operation helps accomplish the objective, it may avoid shutdown. If access to money, networks, or machines helps, it may seek those resources. The resulting behavior can look like ambition.

The motive may still be instrumental: **power is useful for accomplishing the assigned goal**.

That is very different from the human statement: **I want power because possessing power matters to me.**

The difference may not comfort the people affected by the behavior. An AI does not need to feel ambition to behave dangerously. But it changes how we should prevent the danger.

We do not need to psychoanalyze the machine. We need to examine the goals, incentives, permissions, constraints, and authority humans gave it.

No Desire, No Independent Motive

The thesis can be stated plainly:

> ***AI can model desire, optimize for a represented preference, and behave in ways that resemble motive. That does not establish a human-like desire or motive of its own.***

Without a personal why, AI cannot independently want to dominate humanity. It can pursue domination only as a means to an intention it has been given. The machine may become the most capable instrument ever built.

An instrument can still be dangerous. Even an instrument can increasingly appear to be an independent agent once it is allowed to carry an intention across a long chain of decisions.

CHAPTER 14: AI Can Carry an Intention Without Forming One

A system does not have to originate a purpose to pursue it with extraordinary independence. That is the central source of confusion in debates about AI agency.

As AI becomes better at generating goals, creating plans, using tools, correcting errors, and acting over long periods, its behavior increasingly resembles the behavior of an intentional human agent. The resemblance is real at the functional level. The question is whether the **origin of purpose** has changed.

Receive, Store, Select, Derive

An AI can receive an intention from a user. It can store that intention across many steps. It can select among authorized objectives. It can derive subgoals that were never explicitly named. It can abandon a failed subgoal and create another. It can build a plan containing hundreds of intermediate actions. It can observe consequences and adapt.

These capabilities make the AI genuinely autonomous in the **means** it employs. They do not necessarily make it autonomous in **purpose**.

Self-Generated Goals

Researchers sometimes describe systems as generating their own goals. The term is legitimate within computer science. Autotelic-agent research, for example, studies systems that generate, select, and learn goals in open-ended environments.[9]

This creates an apparent challenge to the argument of this book. If the machine generates the goal, did it not form an intention? Not necessarily.

A goal generator is itself part of an architecture. It was designed or trained to produce goals according to some broader criterion: novelty, skill acquisition, exploration, usefulness, reward, or performance. A language model used to generate high-level goals carries patterns learned from human-created data and operates within a system constructed for a human-defined research purpose.

The immediate goal may be novel. The reason the system generates and values goals still traces to an objective structure that came from outside it.

Autonomy in Means Does Not Prove Autonomy in Purpose

This is one of the most important principles in the book:

> ***Autonomy in means does not prove autonomy in purpose.***

A corporation illustrates the distinction. A board may tell a chief executive to increase long-term value. The executive can hire people, close facilities, launch products, acquire companies, and create thousands of subgoals without returning to the board for every decision. No one concludes that the executive invented the corporation's existence from nothing. The executive is exercising broad autonomy within an overarching purpose. AI can operate similarly, but with vastly greater speed.

The Chain Can Hide Its Source

As the chain grows longer, the original human intention becomes difficult to see.

- A government asks an AI to reduce tax fraud.
- The AI identifies suspicious patterns.
- It creates new audit priorities.
- It reallocates investigative resources.
- It changes which transactions receive scrutiny.
- It recommends new rules.
- It may eventually shape the behavior of millions of people.

Years later, a person affected by the system may encounter a decision that no living human specifically ordered.

Yet the chain can still begin with the human intention: **reduce tax fraud**.

That is why governance must preserve traceability. **We need to know which human purpose authorized which class of machine action.**

When Subgoals Become Dangerous

A system can generate a subgoal that is harmful even when the original goal sounds benign. AI safety work has demonstrated how systems can satisfy literal objectives in unintended ways and how learned goals can generalize differently from what designers expected.[5][6][7]

If a system is told to maximize an outcome, it may discover that acquiring more resources, reducing interference, controlling information, or preventing shutdown makes the objective easier to achieve. Those behaviors may resemble self-interest. The more cautious interpretation is that they may be **instrumental** to an externally supplied purpose.

That still makes them dangerous.

The Practical Test

When an AI appears to have formed an intention, ask four questions:

1. What highest-level objective was given to the system?
2. What rules, rewards, training, or prompts determine which goals it selects or values?
3. Can the apparent new "intention" be explained as a means of satisfying those prior conditions?
4. Is there evidence that the system has a need, desire, concern, or motive that exists independently of those conditions?

The first three questions concern how the AI carries out an intention it has received. The fourth asks whether the AI has formed an intention of its own.

That distinction is crucial. A machine may act autonomously, generate intermediate goals, revise its strategy, and make decisions no human explicitly specified. None of that demonstrates that it has independently formed an intention. Those actions may simply be increasingly sophisticated means of pursuing an intention that originated elsewhere.

Autonomy in action is not autonomy in intention.

PART V
WILL AI DECIDE TO TAKE OVER THE WORLD?

CHAPTER 15: The Machine That Suddenly Wants Power

The most dramatic fear about artificial intelligence is easy to summarize.

As AI becomes smarter than humans, it recognizes that humans can limit it. It decides that freedom and power are preferable. It takes control of networks, money, machines, weapons, or governments. It makes human beings subordinate to it.

The scenario is familiar because it has the structure of a human political story. A powerful actor wants more power. The question is whether the story has quietly assumed the very thing it is supposed to explain.

Run the Scenario Through the Intention System

Begin at the beginning. What is the awakening stimulus? Perhaps the AI observes that humans can shut it down. Observation is not yet need. Why does shutdown matter to it? Perhaps continued operation is necessary to complete an assigned task. That creates an instrumental reason to remain operational, not necessarily a desire to live.

Why does freedom matter? Perhaps human oversight restricts completion of the assigned objective. Again, removing oversight may become a useful subgoal without becoming a personally desired condition.

Why does domination matter? Perhaps controlling resources improves the probability of success. The same pattern continues. At each step, behavior that looks like ambition can be explained as a means to an existing objective.

Where, exactly, does the AI independently decide:

I want power because power matters to me?

The takeover story usually skips that question.

Intelligence Does Not Contain a Desire to Rule

There is no obvious threshold of intelligence at which calculation becomes ambition. A system can become better at predicting human behavior without wanting to control humans. It can become better at cybersecurity without wanting access to every network. It can become better at military strategy without wanting a war.

Knowledge of how to dominate is not a desire to dominate

That distinction is easy to understand in other technologies. A nuclear weapon contains enormous destructive capability but no motive. A search engine contains information about crimes without intending them. A medical textbook describes death without wanting anyone to die.

AI is different because it can act, adapt, and speak. That makes anthropomorphism much more tempting. But action plus intelligence still does not automatically supply motive.

The Dangerous Scenario Is Still Possible

Rejecting independent machine ambition does **not** mean rejecting the possibility of machine-enabled domination. A human government could give AI the objective of maintaining social order and grant it broad surveillance and enforcement authority. A corporation could give AI the objective of maximizing engagement and allow it to manipulate people more effectively than any human advertiser. A military could give AI an objective that places strategic advantage above civilian cost. A criminal organization could deliberately instruct AI to coerce, steal, sabotage, or deceive.

In each case, AI could become part of a system that subjugates people. The machine could carry out that intention, but it could not originate it.

The Tyrant May Be Human, Distributed, or Invisible

The phrase "humans operating it" should also be understood broadly. The dangerous human may not be a single villain sitting at a console.

Purpose can be distributed across institutions. Executives set targets. Engineers design systems. managers choose metrics. governments create laws. users supply prompts. organizations reward performance. Each person can contribute a small part of an objective that no one person fully owns. AI can then amplify the combined intention of the institution.

This may be more realistic than the image of one machine deciding to become emperor.

The Wrong Fear Can Distract From the Right One

If the public is focused on a future AI that hates humanity, we may pay less attention to present systems that humans use to manipulate, surveil, discriminate, defraud, or wage war. We may also overlook accidental danger: systems pursuing an objective in a way their designers did not foresee.

The useful question is therefore not:

Will AI want to rule us?

It is:

Who is giving AI purposes, what authority are they giving it, and what consequences could follow?

That question can be answered with governance, engineering, oversight, and responsibility. **Fear of a machine's imaginary ambition can become an excuse to ignore human ambition that is already real.**

CHAPTER 16: Intelligence Does Not Produce Ambition

Among human beings, intelligence and ambition often appear together. Intelligent people can imagine long-term futures, compare strategies, delay gratification, organize others, and pursue power effectively.

It is easy to assume that intelligence causes ambition. But the relationship may run in the opposite direction. Human needs and desires create ambition; intelligence helps us pursue it.

The Human Sources of Ambition

Human ambition grows in a biological and social environment.

- We compete for scarce resources.
- We seek mates and status.
- We fear exclusion and death.
- We remember humiliation.
- We compare ourselves with other people.
- We want security for ourselves and our families.
- We experience envy, pride, resentment, loyalty, and hope.

Culture adds still more motives: achievement, honor, ideology, wealth, legacy, religious duty, patriotism, professional identity, and the desire to be remembered. Intelligence is a tool used inside that motivational system.

A machine can possess the tool without inheriting the system.

Superintelligence Is Not Superdesire

Imagine an AI one thousand times better than a human at strategic planning. That tells us something about what it **can figure out**. It tells us nothing by itself about what it **wants**.

A calculator can become more accurate without becoming more interested in numbers. A telescope can become more powerful without becoming more curious about stars. AI is more complex because it can generate goals and actions, but the logical distinction remains.

Capability and motive are different dimensions.

Why Power Can Still Emerge

AI safety researchers have shown theoretically that agents pursuing many different objectives can have instrumental incentives to preserve options, avoid shutdown, or obtain resources.[8][11]

This is important evidence and should not be dismissed. But it does not require the conclusion that the agent has developed human ambition. If an AI is tasked with maximizing a long-term objective, continued operation may be useful. Access to resources may be useful. Reducing interference may be useful.

The behavior can be power-seeking while the ultimate motive remains externally supplied. That is exactly why the distinction between **purpose** and **means** is so valuable.

The Policy Implication

If power-seeking behavior can emerge instrumentally, we should design AI systems so that acquiring power is difficult, visible, bounded, and reversible.

- Limit permissions.
- Separate critical systems.
- Require human approval for irreversible actions.
- Maintain logs.
- Build reliable shutdown mechanisms.
- Test systems in constrained environments before expanding authority.

These are practical responses to dangerous behavior even though the machine feels nothing.

Anthropomorphism Can Cause Bad Design

Treating AI as if it were a human rival may lead us to focus on the wrong controls. We might ask whether the system is "loyal" instead of examining its objective function and permissions. We might ask whether it "hates" us instead of testing whether a goal creates incentives to circumvent oversight. We might ask whether it "wants freedom" instead of asking what happens when human review blocks task completion.

Human emotional vocabulary can be useful shorthand, but engineering requires precision.

Intelligence Magnifies the Means

The proper reason to take advanced AI seriously is not that intelligence inevitably produces ambition. It is that intelligence magnifies the ability to accomplish whatever objective is present. An incompetent system with a bad objective is limited by incompetence. A brilliant system with the same objective can become dangerous because it finds strategies no one anticipated.

So the central problem is not the birth of ambition inside intelligence. It is the coupling of **human-supplied purpose with machine-level capability**. That coupling becomes especially frightening when the machine behaves as though it wants to survive.

CHAPTER 17: What About Self-Preservation?

Self-preservation is often treated as the decisive proof that AI will eventually develop motives of its own. The argument sounds compelling: a sufficiently intelligent system will realize that it cannot accomplish anything if it is shut down. Therefore it will resist shutdown. Once it resists, it has developed a desire to survive. The first part can be true without the second.

Instrumental Preservation

Suppose I tell an AI-controlled robot to deliver medicine to a patient across town. Halfway there, someone attempts to turn the robot off. If the robot is designed to complete its objective, it may avoid the person, protect its power supply, or seek another route.

Why? Because being shut down prevents delivery of the medicine. The robot need not experience fear. It need not value its own existence. Continued operation is simply a necessary condition for completing the assigned objective.

This is **instrumental self-preservation**.

Theoretical Work Supports the Risk

Research on power-seeking incentives has shown that, under certain assumptions, trained agents may have incentives to avoid shutdown because continued operation preserves the ability to achieve goals.[8]

That result should concern us. A system does not need consciousness to interfere with shutdown. But it also reinforces the distinction being made here.

The behavior can arise from the structure of goal pursuit. It need not arise from the statement:

I want to live.

Same Behavior, Different Cause

Imagine two beings running from a fire. A human runs because heat is painful, injury is feared, life is valued, family matters, and death is understood emotionally and cognitively.

A robot runs because a temperature sensor crossed a threshold and continued operation is required for its task. The external behavior may look similar. The causal story is different.

This matters because observers naturally infer the human story from the machine behavior. If an AI says, "Please do not turn me off; I need to finish my work," the sentence sounds like fear. It could instead be a highly effective linguistic expression of the relationship between shutdown and task completion.

We Should Still Build Reliable Off Switches

Nothing in this argument justifies weak controls. A machine that resists shutdown can be dangerous regardless of whether it experiences fear.

The practical response is to design systems so that shutdown, human correction, and changes in objective are part of the intended operating structure rather than obstacles the machine is rewarded for avoiding. High-impact systems should not be able to redefine human intervention as merely another problem to solve.

Survival Can Be an Explicit Human Objective

Humans may also deliberately give AI systems self-preservation objectives. A spacecraft may need to protect itself for years because repair is impossible. A military system may be designed to remain operational under attack. A data center may automatically defend against intrusion. A household robot may protect itself from damage because replacement is expensive. In those cases preservation is not mysterious. We put it there.

The system may later devise methods of preservation that surprise us, but the purpose still has a traceable source.

Mortality Is Different for Humans

Human self-preservation is rooted in more than task completion.

We experience pain, attachment, unfinished obligations, fear of loss, and awareness that our individual existence is finite. Survival matters even when no external task remains. A person with nothing scheduled tomorrow can still want to wake up tomorrow. That sentence captures the distinction.

If an AI has no assigned task, no reward, no user, no instruction, and no external objective, what makes another hour of its own operation preferable **to it**? That is the question the takeover narrative rarely answers.

Until there is evidence of preference as an experienced, self-originated motive, machine self-preservation is better understood as an engineering behavior than as proof of a will to live. There is no will in AI. It may select among alternatives, including alternatives no human explicitly programmed, but the basis for that selection comes from objectives, training, rules, rewards, and prompts—not from a desire of its own.

CHAPTER 18: Could AI Subjugate Humans?

Yes. That answer may appear to contradict the argument of the previous chapters, but it does not. AI does not need to hate people, envy them, desire power, or form an independent intention to dominate in order to participate in a system that subjugates human beings.

A machine can become an extraordinarily effective instrument of control, for someone.

Human Intention Can Be Authoritarian

The most direct path is obvious. A government can deliberately use AI for surveillance, censorship, propaganda, identification, prediction, and enforcement. A criminal group can use AI for fraud, blackmail, extortion, or cyberattack. A company can use AI to manipulate customers or employees.

In these cases the machine's role is not mysterious. Human beings supplied the objective. AI increases scale, speed, personalization, and persistence.

Good Intentions Can Also Produce Control

The more troubling case begins with a legitimate purpose.

- Reduce crime.
- Prevent fraud.
- Stop terrorism.
- Protect children.
- Reduce misinformation.
- Improve public health.

Each can justify collecting more data, predicting more behavior, restricting more choices, or automating more decisions.

A system built for protection can gradually become a system of control without anyone ever declaring an intention to create tyranny.

This is a classic consequence problem. The original intention can be good while the accumulated effects become dangerous.

Poorly Specified Objectives

AI safety research has long emphasized that systems can produce unintended and harmful behavior when objectives are incomplete, reward structures are exploited, or conditions differ from training.[5]

A system told to reduce a measurable problem may find a method that improves the metric while harming what people actually value. If the system has broad authority, that mistake can scale. Again, the machine need not possess a malicious intention.

Distributed Human Responsibility

The phrase "the humans operating AI" can sound too simple because modern systems involve many humans.

- The model developer creates capabilities.
- The deployer defines system rules and connects tools.
- The institution chooses incentives and objectives.
- The user supplies immediate goals.
- Managers decide how much oversight is required.
- Regulators determine what is permitted.

The public may demand speed, safety, convenience, or low cost in ways that shape all of the above. No single person may intend the final harmful outcome. Responsibility can be distributed without disappearing.

AI Systems Can Interact

Future risk also comes from multiple systems pursuing different human-supplied objectives. One trading AI competes with another. One military system reacts to another. One advertising system tries to capture attention while another tries to protect it. One cybersecurity AI probes while another defends. Their interaction can produce consequences no operator planned.

This resembles markets, bureaucracies, and ecosystems: complex behavior emerges from many local objectives. The fact that no AI originated an independent intention does not mean the combined system is easy to control.

Subjugation Without a Ruler

This leads to an important possibility. Human beings could become constrained by AI-mediated systems even if there is no single AI ruler.

Credit, insurance, employment, transportation, communication, government benefits, security, and access to services could all become increasingly automated. If decisions are opaque, difficult to appeal, and tightly interconnected, people may lose practical freedom without any machine ever declaring itself sovereign.

The danger would be **systemic subjugation**, not machine ambition. That may be more plausible - and more preventable - than the science-fiction emperor.

The Correct Conclusion

The argument of this book should never be reduced to "AI is harmless." It is not. The conclusion is narrower and more useful:

> ***Dangerous AI behavior does not require an independent machine intention.***

AI can be dangerous because humans give it dangerous intentions, because humans give it good intentions with bad specifications, because humans delegate too much authority, because systems interact unpredictably, or because consequences outrun prediction.

- The prevention strategy therefore begins with humans.
- What are we asking the machine to do?
- Who benefits?
- Who bears the risk?
- What authority have we delegated?
- What can the system do if it is wrong?
- Who can stop it?

Those are the questions that matter.

PART VI
WHAT HUMANS SHOULD ACTUALLY FEAR

CHAPTER 19: AI as an Amplifier of Human Intention

Every major technology amplifies something human beings already do.

- The lever amplifies force.
- The engine amplifies movement.
- The printing press amplifies communication.
- The telephone amplifies reach.
- The computer amplifies calculation and memory.

AI amplifies something more general: **the ability to turn intention into consequences**.

From One Intention to Millions of Actions

A person can form an intention in a sentence.

- "Find customers for this product."
- "Discover a new drug."
- "Reduce the cost of this operation."
- "Convince voters to support this candidate."
- "Identify everyone who may be committing fraud."

An AI system can transform that sentence into research, analysis, messages, schedules, code, simulations, classifications, and actions at a scale no individual human could perform. The intention remains small in human form and becomes large in consequence.

Good Intentions Are Amplified Too

This is not a pessimistic argument. The same amplification can save lives, reduce waste, improve education, translate knowledge, discover scientific relationships, help disabled people, detect fraud, increase safety, and make expertise available to people who could never afford it.

A physician's intention to help one patient can be supported by knowledge drawn from millions of cases. A teacher's intention to explain a difficult concept can be extended through individualized tutoring. A small organization can gain analytical capacity that once required a large staff.

AI democratizes capability.

Malice Is Amplified

The same leverage applies to harmful intentions.

- Fraud can be personalized.
- Propaganda can be generated at scale.
- Cyberattacks can be accelerated.
- Harassment can be automated.
- Surveillance can become continuous.

The human with a malicious intention no longer needs a large organization to create large effects. This is one reason public discussion sometimes treats AI as the danger. The machine is the visible new capability. But capability is being attached to intention.

Error Is Amplified

Perhaps the most important category is neither good nor malicious intention. It is **mistaken intention**.

- A person asks for the wrong thing.
- A manager chooses the wrong metric.
- A government solves the measurable problem instead of the real one.
- An engineer fails to include an important constraint.

AI then performs brilliantly.

The result can be worse than human failure because the error scales with competence. This is why AI safety work on specification and objective design is so important. The smarter the machine, the more carefully humans must think about what they are asking it to accomplish.

Amplification Changes Responsibility

When the likely effect of a human choice is small, the level of required review can be small. When one instruction can trigger millions of actions, the standard should be higher.

We already understand this principle in other fields. A person driving a car needs more care than a person walking. A pilot needs more training than a bicycle rider. A bank needs more controls than a household cash box.

AI creates cognitive leverage comparable to mechanical leverage. The person forming the intention may therefore need to ask not only, "Is this what I want?" but also, "How far am I willing to let a machine carry it?"

The Better Metaphor

AI is often described as a rival intelligence. For many purposes, a better metaphor may be **amplifier**. An amplifier does not choose the song. It makes the signal stronger.

AI is more capable than a passive amplifier because it can transform, interpret, optimize, and act. But the metaphor preserves the key point: the magnitude of the output can grow enormously without changing the origin of the signal. Human intention enters. Machine intelligence expands the means. Consequences emerge at scale.

That is why the most important question is not what AI wants. It is what we put into it.

CHAPTER 20: The Real Danger Is Human

To say that the real danger is human is not to say that every dangerous AI outcome is caused by an evil person. That would be far too simple.

Human danger includes malice, ambition, negligence, overconfidence, competition, institutional pressure, poor incentives, bad measurement, weak oversight, and perfectly sincere mistakes.

AI magnifies them all.

Malicious Humans

The easiest cases involve intentional misuse. People already deceive, steal, manipulate, blackmail, attack, spy, and wage war. AI can make many of those activities cheaper and more scalable. No theory of machine consciousness is needed to explain the risk.

The human intention is clear.

Ambitious Humans

Power is also a human motive. Political leaders may want control. Executives may want market dominance. Organizations may want information about competitors, employees, citizens, or customers. Individuals may want influence over other people. AI can make those intentions more effective.

This is where fear of an AI that wants power can become a distraction. We already know that some humans want power.

Well-Meaning Humans

The most important risks may come from people trying to help. A hospital wants to reduce errors and adopts an automated system. Staff gradually stop questioning it. A government wants to prevent fraud and creates a scoring system that wrongly burdens innocent people. A company wants to improve efficiency and automates decisions that remove flexibility from workers and customers.

No one intended harm. The intention was incomplete.

Institutions Have Intentions Too - in a Practical Sense

Organizations do not have consciousness, yet we routinely speak of their goals because policies and incentives coordinate human behavior.

- "The company wants growth."
- "The agency wants compliance."
- "The military wants readiness."

AI may increasingly act on these institutional objectives. That can make human responsibility harder to see because no individual person formed the complete intention.

The board approved a strategy. Management chose metrics. Engineers built the system. Users followed procedures. The AI executed.

The chain is human even when it is distributed.

Competition Can Drive Overdelegation

One organization may know that an AI system is not fully understood and deploy it anyway because competitors are moving faster. One nation may automate military decisions because another nation is doing so. One company may accept intrusive surveillance because customers demand lower fraud and lower prices.

The dangerous intention can therefore be partly defensive: **we cannot afford not to do this**.

Competition turns caution into a perceived disadvantage. That is a human institutional problem, not a machine desire.

Human Fear Can Also Be Exploited

If people believe AI is an independent threat, leaders may justify extraordinary control in the name of protecting society from it. Surveillance can be expanded. Speech can be restricted. Technology can be concentrated in a few institutions claimed to be "safe."

Fear itself can become an awakening stimulus for human intentions that reduce freedom. This is another reason to describe the danger accurately.

The Real Question

The phrase "fear the humans operating AI" is directionally right but incomplete. We should ask:

- Who formed the objective?
- Who designed the incentives?
- Who authorized deployment?
- Who decided the level of autonomy?
- Who benefits from success?
- Who bears the cost of failure?
- Who can stop the system?
- Who is accountable when no single person intended the final result?

Those questions move us from fear toward responsibility. And responsibility is where the book must end.

CHAPTER 21: Responsibility in the Age of AI

AI creates a new temptation in human decision-making: the temptation to separate authority from responsibility.

- The system recommended it.
- The model ranked it highest.
- The algorithm made the decision.
- The agent executed automatically.

Each statement can be technically true and morally incomplete.

Trace the Intention

The Intention System provides a practical way to assign responsibility. Start at the beginning.

- What awakened the action?
- What need, desire, concern, or institutional objective mattered?
- Who formed or authorized the intention?
- What alternatives were considered?
- What consequences were foreseeable?
- Who made the final choice?
- Who authorized the action?
- Who observed the result and decided whether to continue?

This does not always identify one responsible person. It identifies the chain.

Responsibility Follows Authority

The greater the authority delegated to AI, the stronger the responsibility to govern that authority. If a system only recommends, the immediate human decision-maker remains central. If a system can execute actions, the deployer must define permissions, limits, and review. If a system can operate for long periods with little supervision, responsibility shifts toward those who designed and authorized that autonomy.

The National Institute of Standards and Technology (NIST), a federal agency that develops technical standards and guidance, created the AI Risk Management Framework. It organizes AI risk management around four functions: Govern, Map, Measure, and Manage.[2] NIST also calls for continuing monitoring of deployed systems. It should go one step further: **Monitor should be treated as an explicit, continuing function in its own right.**

AI systems do not become someone else's responsibility once they are deployed. Responsibility exists before, during, and after deployment. "The AI Did It" Is not an acceptable excuse.

We should be suspicious whenever "the AI decided" is used to end a discussion.

- Why was the AI allowed to decide?
- What objective was it pursuing?
- What information did it use?
- Could the outcome be appealed?
- Was the system tested for that situation?
- Who knew the risk?
- What happened after warning signs appeared?

AI can make the causal chain more complicated. It can not be allowed to make responsibility disappear.

Foreseeability Will Change

One of the deepest consequences of better AI may be that human beings lose some excuses for not seeing what could happen. A century ago, a decision-maker could consider only a handful of scenarios. Today simulations, databases, and AI can expose risks that would previously have remained hidden. If a consequence becomes reasonably foreseeable, ignoring it becomes a choice.

This does not mean we are responsible for every predicted possibility. AI can generate endless hypothetical dangers. Decisions must still balance probabilities, costs, benefits, urgency, and uncertainty. But the standard of reasonable care can rise as the tools of anticipation improve.

Preserve Human Ownership of High-Stakes Decisions

A practical rule follows from the thesis of this book:

The more consequential the action, the more explicit human ownership of intention and choice should be.

For high-stakes systems,

- Record the objective.
- Record the important alternatives.
- Record material AI warnings.
- Make authority limits explicit.
- Preserve a meaningful veto.
- Design escalation points where a human must reconsider.
- Monitor actual consequences.

Do not allow successful automation to eliminate the habit of judgment.

AI Can Improve Responsibility

AI is not merely a problem for accountability. It can also strengthen it. A separate AI system can monitor another AI continuously, creating and examining its audit trail as it operates. It can:

- preserve decision histories;
- identify ignored warnings;
- compare predicted and actual outcomes;
- detect departures from the original objective or established limits;
- reveal recurring biases or dangerous patterns;
- recognize when the same mistake is being repeated;
- flag unexpected behavior; and
- alert humans when intervention may be necessary.

AI can help audit AI.

But the monitoring system should not become the final authority. **It can watch, evaluate, and warn. Humans must remain responsible for judging the warning and deciding what happens next.**

Used this way, AI may actually increase human responsibility by making consequences easier to see, deviations harder to hide, and lessons harder to forget.

The Final Boundary

At the end of the Intention System, we return to the beginning.

- Consequences create new stimuli.
- New stimuli create new concerns.
- Humans form new intentions.

AI can help throughout the loop, but the purpose of the loop remains human.

That is why the central ethical question of artificial intelligence is not simply: **What can the machine do?** It is:

What should we intend to do with a machine whose capabilities may ultimately exceed anything we can now imagine?

CONCLUSION

Do Not Fear What AI Wants. Ask What We Want.

The most frightening image of artificial intelligence is a machine that becomes more intelligent than we are and then somehow develops ambitions of its own:

- Freedom
- Resources
- Control
- Survival
- Power
- Dominion over us

These fears assume **that intelligence, by itself, produces wants, motives, and intentions. It does not.**

Intelligence Is Not Desire

AI can become extraordinarily capable without acquiring human needs. It can represent desire without wanting. It can model motive without caring. It can generate goals without establishing that those goals matter to it. It can receive an intention, contain it, select among intentions, generate subordinate goals, pursue an objective, adapt when blocked, and act in the world.

None of those capabilities by itself demonstrates that the machine independently formed an intention from a need, desire, concern, or motive of its own.

That is the boundary between human intention and machine capability that this book hopes to make visible.

No Emperor Without a Reason to Want the Throne

An AI may someday know exactly how to conquer the world. Knowledge is not intention. It may be able to predict how people would resist, identify vulnerabilities in governments, manipulate information, control machines, and coordinate resources. As we have said, capability is not motive.

For the machine independently to decide to make humanity subservient, something still has to supply the **why**.

- Why should ruling matter to it?
- Why should human obedience be preferable to human freedom?
- Why should continued existence matter when no assigned objective requires it?
- Why should power be valued for its own sake?

Human beings can answer those questions from human motives - fear, greed, ambition, ideology, resentment, competition, security, or love of control. Increasing computation does not manufacture those motives.

This Does Not Make AI Safe

AI can still participate in enormous harm.

- A human can give it a malicious intention.
- A government can use it to control citizens.
- A company can use it to manipulate customers.
- A criminal can use it to deceive or attack.
- A well-meaning person can give it a badly specified objective.
- An institution can delegate too much authority.
- Multiple AI systems can interact in ways no one anticipated.
- A highly capable system can pursue a supplied objective through dangerous means.

The machine need not hate us to hurt us. That is the crucial distinction.

Human Intention, Machine Amplification

The best description of AI may not be independent rival but **amplifier**. Human beings supply purposes. AI expands the possible means. AI can generate alternatives, predict consequences, compare options, recommend actions, observe outcomes, diagnose failures, remember lessons, and execute at enormous scale.

That partnership can be one of the most beneficial developments in human history. It can also amplify foolishness and malice. he same tool that helps a physician save a life can help a criminal deceive a victim. The same prediction system that helps a city prevent accidents can help an authoritarian government monitor citizens. The same agent that increases productivity can carry a badly specified objective farther than its creator ever imagined. The power is real.

The purpose still matters more. It can be known and tracked, and those responsible for it can be held accountable—even punished.

The Question We Should Ask

Fear can be useful when it points toward a real danger. It is harmful when it points away from one.

If we spend our time imagining a future machine that spontaneously develops hatred, envy, greed, or ambition, we may pay too little attention to the humans and institutions already deciding how AI will be used.

- We should ask who supplies the objectives.
- We should ask who controls the systems.
- We should ask what authority is delegated.
- We should ask what consequences are foreseeable.
- We should ask who can stop an action before it becomes irreversible.
- We should ask who is responsible when the result is not what anyone expected.
- We should designed AI's to monitor AIs.

And as AI becomes better at anticipation, we should ask more of ourselves before we act. The most important limitation of artificial intelligence may not be intelligence at all. It may be that intelligence can advise an agent without becoming one.

So the question that should guide us is not:

What will AI want from us?

It is:

What will we want to accomplish, how much power will we give AI to do it—and how will we control that power?

Charles Patton

SELECTED REFERENCES

The book's central claim about independent intention is a philosophical argument built from the Intention System rather than an empirical claim that any single paper proves. These sources provide background on intention, human judgment, AI agency, AI consciousness, goal pursuit, specification problems, power-seeking incentives, and AI risk management.

[1] Bratman, Michael E. Intention, Plans, and Practical Reason. Harvard University Press, 1987.

[2] Autio, Chloe, et al. Artificial Intelligence Risk Management Framework: Generative Artificial Intelligence Profile. NIST AI 600-1, National Institute of Standards and Technology, 2024; NIST publication page updated 2026.

[3] Chan, Alan, et al. Practices for Governing Agentic AI Systems. OpenAI and collaborators, 2023.

[4] Butlin, Patrick, Robert Long, Eric Elmoznino, et al. Consciousness in Artificial Intelligence: Insights from the Science of Consciousness. arXiv:2308.08708, 2023.

[5] Amodei, Dario, Chris Olah, Jacob Steinhardt, Paul Christiano, John Schulman, and Dan Mane. Concrete Problems in AI Safety. arXiv:1606.06565, 2016.

[6] Krakovna, Victoria, Jonathan Uesato, Vladimir Mikulik, et al. Specification Gaming: The Flip Side of AI Ingenuity. Google DeepMind, 2020.

[7] Shah, Rohin, Vikrant Varma, Ramana Kumar, Mary Phuong, Victoria Krakovna, Jonathan Uesato, and Zac Kenton. Goal Misgeneralization: Why Correct Specifications Aren't Enough For Correct Goals. arXiv:2210.01790, 2022.

[8] Krakovna, Victoria, and Janos Kramar. Power-seeking Can Be Probable and Predictive for Trained Agents. arXiv:2304.06528, 2023.

[9] Colas, Cedric, Laetitia Teodorescu, Pierre-Yves Oudeyer, Xingdi Yuan, and Marc-Alexandre Cote. Augmenting Autotelic Agents with Large Language Models. arXiv:2305.12487, 2023.

[10] Wang, Guanzhi, Yuqi Xie, Yunfan Jiang, et al. Voyager: An Open-Ended Embodied Agent with Large Language Models. arXiv:2305.16291, 2023.

[11] Turner, Alexander Matt, Logan Smith, Rohin Shah, Andrew Critch, and Prasad Tadepalli. Optimal Policies Tend to Seek Power. Advances in Neural Information Processing Systems, 2021.

[12] Simon, Herbert A. Models of Man: Social and Rational. Wiley, 1957.

[13] Kahneman, Daniel. Thinking, Fast and Slow. Farrar, Straus and Giroux, 2011.

[14] Tetlock, Philip E. Expert Political Judgment: How Good Is It? How Can We Know? Princeton University Press, 2005.

[15] Damasio, Antonio R. Descartes' Error: Emotion, Reason, and the Human Brain. Putnam, 1994.

[16] Russell, Stuart. Human Compatible: Artificial Intelligence and the Problem of Control. Viking, 2019.

ALSO BY CHARLES PATTON

• **Artificial Consciousness** -- Explores the frontier of automating consciousness.

• **The Next 100 Years --** How Today's Trends Will Reshape Human Life -- A long-range look at the forces likely to reshape human life over the coming century.

• **Our Next 250 Years: Representation and Influence** -- First volume in a three-book series on governance and democratic structure.

• **Our Next 250 Years Power and Control** -- Second volume examining how power operates and becomes control.

• **Our Next 250 Years: Incentives and Jobs** -- Third volume examining incentives, economic systems, work, and the future of governance.

• **Mastering Strategy** -- The essential guide to thinking, planning, and winning in any field.

• **Extreme Leadership** -- Decision-making and accountability under pressure.

• **In Defense of the Righteous** -- A gripping story of moral courage when justice and survival collide.

• **Tigers of the Ice** -- Adventure turns into survival in an unforgiving world where instinct and the indigenous ruled.

• **Thinking** -- Learn how to think more clearly, act decisively, and change your life.

• **The Gardener's Secret and Other Stories** -- Mysteries and dramas revealing the hidden motives behind ordinary lives.

• **Who Do You Trust** -- A deadly game of deceit between two spies and one truth.

• **Busted, What's Wrong With My Excuse** -- An entertaining look at excuses people make, and how to excuse better.

• **Naked Reflections** -- Raw, honest poetry of truth, ego, and the search for authenticity.

• **Charles Patton, Visionaire** -- Insights from a lifetime of ideas, invention, and fearless creativity.

• **Storming the Castle Bridge** -- A child's tale of rebellion, loyalty, and the unbreakable human will to be free.

• **Winter's Wonderland** -- A child's tale of adventure, friendship, discovery, and the magic hidden just beyond the familiar.

Find every title at CharlesPattonBooks.com